Dedication

To my husband Guangyou,
our children Caleb, Christine and Charissa,
and my dad and mum, Charles and Lily

Contents

Sugar & Spice & Everything Nice

Come On & Celebrate!

Acknowledgements

First of all, I would like to thank God for giving me the opportunity, passion and inspiration for this baking journey. It is something I would never have expected three years ago. He is truly behind every one of my creations.

I would like to thank my husband and best friend for always being by my side, for his understanding and for constantly providing insights into my creations.

I am grateful to my parents for their unceasing love and support. Without them, I would not have been able to pursue my passion for making creative chiffon cakes. (Thanks dad and mum!)

I am also extremely blessed to have my children's support. They (and their interests) are the inspiration behind many of my creations.

I would also like to thank my important mummy friends-cum-baking *kakis*, especially Phay Shing and Christine and Charissa's groups for their constant support, friendship and encouragement. It has been a wonderful journey!

I would like to thank Lydia, my editor, for being the best editor I could ever have asked for! She is such a joy to work with, always understanding, accommodating, brilliant and fun!

I would also like to thank Benson the designer for making everything look so pretty in the book, and Hongde the photographer for his awesome artwork, styling and professionalism.

Thanks also to Phoon Huat & Co Pte Ltd and Chew's Group Limited, my favourite ingredient suppliers, for their kind and generous support of this second book.

Introduction

I started baking chiffon cakes more than three years ago, and it amazes me what can be achieved with some creativity. Chiffon cakes can take on all sorts of fun and exciting shapes, and be patterned and decorated to rival even fondant and cream cakes in terms of look and design, without compromising on taste or texture.

In my first book, *Creative Baking: Chiffon Cakes*, I shared a collection of cute chiffon cake pops and cupcakes, patterned and decorated piñata chiffon cakes and rainbow and hidden surprise chiffon cakes. As a first-time cookbook author, I didn't know what to expect, but the support I received was overwhelming! All who picked up the book and tried the recipes loved the ideas, the colours and designs, and most importantly, the taste and texture of the cakes they created in their own kitchens. And they wanted to try more recipes, hence this book you now hold in your hands.

In this second book, I share even more creative ideas with 3D pattern cakes and a host of new shapes. There is also a special collection of festive cakes suitable for Christmas, Chinese New Year and even Halloween. With feedback received from friends and other home bakers, I have also expanded the Chiffon Cake 101 section and Troubleshooting Guide to guide you as you embark on your creative baking journey.

Thank you for your continued support and encouragement. May you bring smiles to the faces of your loved ones with this collection of chiffon cake creations. Have fun baking!

Susanne

1
2

Basic Tools & Equipment

1 Chiffon Tube Pans

Chiffon cakes are traditionally baked in tube pans as this type of cake is very delicate and needs to cling to the centre tube and the sides of the pan to enable rising during baking, and prevent sinking while cooling. For this reason, chiffon tube pans must not be greased and non-stick tube pans cannot be used. Standard chiffon tube pan sizes are 15 cm, 18 cm, 20 cm and 23 cm.

When baking single tone chiffon cakes, the capacity is generally:

15-cm chiffon tube pan: 2 egg yolks and 3 egg whites

18-cm chiffon tube pan: 3 egg yolks and 4 egg whites

20-cm chiffon tube pan: 5 egg yolks and 7 egg whites

23-cm chiffon tube pan: 6 egg yolks and 8 egg whites

Dual tone or rainbow chiffon cakes usually require an additional egg or two due to loss while transferring the batter between mixing bowls.

Chiffon tube pans must be inverted during the sensitive stage of cooling so that gravity can help pull the cake to its maximum height before the cake structure stabilizes.

2 Other Types of Moulds

Through experimenting, I have found that chiffon cakes can be baked in a variety of moulds, provided that the volume is not too large, and the chiffon cake is able to grip on to the surface. Some examples are glass bowls, shaped metal moulds, silicone moulds, paper cones and eggshells.

Moulds with a bigger volume such as glass bowls, metal moulds and silicone Bundts are preferably inverted during the cooling stage to prevent the cake from sinking. For smaller moulds, inverting does not make a difference to the height of the cooled cake.

To prepare eggshell moulds, make a hole on one side of an egg and drain the contents. Wash the shell thoroughly and peel away the white membrane from the inside of the shell.

In these recipes, I also use shallow baking pans for baking the layer chiffon cakes used in decorating the cakes. The size of the shallow baking pans used will depend on the type of decoration required. When very little decoration is required, the smallest pan size (15-cm x 15-cm) is typically used.

3

Baking Paper

Also known as parchment or greaseproof paper, baking paper is used to line baking pans when making sheet cakes to enable the cake to be removed easily from the pan. Baking paper should not be used in chiffon tube pans, glass bowls or metal moulds.

4

Kitchen Scale

As the amount of each ingredient used in making chiffon cakes can be small, and some recipes also call for accuracy down to 1 g, a digital weighing scale is recommended. Digital scales are also preferred for the tare function which enables the scale to discount the weight of the container and only display the weight of the contents. This is useful when the recipe calls for the batter to be divided into a number of portions.

5

Measuring Spoons

Measuring spoons come in a set: 1/8 tsp, 1/4 tsp, 1/2 tsp, 1 tsp and 1 Tbsp. These spoons can be used for measuring both liquid and dry ingredients. For liquid ingredients, fill the spoon to the brim. For dry ingredients, fill the spoon until it is full, then level it off with a spatula or knife.

6

Sieve

Sifting dry ingredients such as flour, baking powder or cocoa powder using a fine mesh sieve helps to break up any lumps in the flour and aerate it. This also makes the flour lighter, helping it to be more easily incorporated into the batter, to create a cake that is lighter, finer and more delicate in texture.

7

Electric Mixer

A handheld electric mixer is recommended for mixing the egg yolk batter, to help incorporate air into the batter. When mixing the egg yolk batter, set the electric mixer to low or medium speed.

For whisking the meringue, both the handheld or stand mixer may be used. The handheld mixer requires high speed to whisk the meringue to firm peaks, so get a handheld mixer with a range of speeds if you are using the same mixer for beating the egg yolks and whisking the egg whites.

Always wash the beater attachment well after mixing the egg yolk batter and ensure it is clean and grease-free before whisking the egg whites, as the presence of grease may affect the foaming properties of the egg whites.

3
4
UNIT
TIME
ON/TARE
6
7

8
9
10
11
12
13
14

8 Mixing Bowls

Have a few mixing bowls of various sizes on hand: small ones for the egg yolk batters and larger ones for the egg whites where the meringue increases many times in volume. The mixing bowl for the meringue must be grease-free and cannot be made from plastic. Metal and glass mixing bowls are recommended for use with the meringue.

9 Pastry Brush

Keep small parts of the cake moist by brushing with a sugar syrup, especially for designs where the assembly requires more time.

10 Silicone Spatula and Silicone Whisk

Folding the meringue into the egg yolk batter requires very gentle mixing, and a flexible silicone spatula or silicone whisk is recommended in combination with gentle unidirectional strokes.

11 Pastry Scraper

This is used to level the batter in the baking pan when baking sheet cakes to ensure the cake is of an even thickness.

12 Cookie Cutters or Plunger Cutters

Cutters in various shapes such as circles, hearts, flowers and stars are used to cut out shapes from the sheet cakes for simple decorations.

13 Oven Thermometer

This is an important tool for monitoring the oven temperature since chiffon cakes are extremely sensitive to changes in temperature, and especially since many recipes call for sequential reduction in temperature and not all ovens may respond similarly. For example, my small oven takes 2 minutes longer to adjust to the temperature change compared to my larger oven. Hence it is extremely important to check for doneness using a skewer.

14 Piping Tips and Piping Bags

2-mm and 3-mm rounded tips are typically used for piping patterns when making decorated chiffon cakes. If you do not have piping tips, improvise by cutting a 2-mm or 3-mm hole at the tip of a disposable piping bag.

1
2
3
4
5
6
7
8
9
10
11

Basic Ingredients

DRY INGREDIENTS

1 **Cake Flour**

In baking chiffon cakes, cake flour is used instead of plain (all-purpose) flour as it has a low protein content and will yield cakes with a softer, finer texture and a more tender crumb. It is also important to sift the cake flour before use to aerate it and remove any lumps in the flour. Sifting will also allows the flour to be more easily mixed into the batter, ensuring that the batter is not over mixed.

2 **Sugar**

Castor sugar is used in the egg yolk batter and meringue in all the recipes in this book. Castor sugar is finer than regular granulated sugar, and will dissolve more quickly. This is especially useful when whisking meringues. Castor sugar is not to be confused with icing or confectioner's sugar, which is ground into powder and sometimes mixed with cornstarch to prevent clumping. Do not use regular granulated sugar or icing sugar in place of castor sugar in these recipes as the texture of the cake will be affected.

3 **Cream of Tartar**

Cream of tartar is used for stabilising egg whites when whisking the meringue. It also helps to increase the heat tolerance and volume of meringue. Cream of tartar is essentially potassium bitartrate, made from tartaric acid which stabilises the meringue. Generally, only $^1/_{16}$ tsp or a pinch of cream of tartar is needed per egg white in making chiffon cakes. Too much cream of tartar will result in the cake tasting sour. Cream of tartar can also be substituted with lemon juice or white vinegar. Replace every $^1/_2$ tsp cream of tartar with 1 tsp lemon juice or white vinegar.

4 **Baking Powder**

Baking powder is usually omitted and not necessary for light and fluffy chiffon cakes if the meringue is correctly whisked and folded. However, there are certain exceptions, such as when a recipe calls for a substantial amount of citrus zest, cocoa powder or red yeast powder, all which have the effect of dampening the batter. We also use baking powder in recipes that call for dense liquid ingredients such as pumpkin purée, black sesame paste and peanut butter etc.

5

Cocoa Powder

There are two types of cocoa powder: natural and Dutch-processed (or alkalised) cocoa powder. Dutch-processed cocoa powder is used in all the recipes in this book and for ease, we will refer to it as cocoa powder.

Both natural and Dutch-processed cocoa powder are made from cocoa beans, but Dutch-processed cocoa beans are soaked in an alkaline solution before being dried, which lowers their acidity, resulting in a darker colour, and also less harsh and richer chocolate flavour. Both types of cocoa powder are commonly used in baking, but when natural cocoa powder is used, baking soda is usually required for the leavening action with the acid which helps the cake rise and also prevent the formation of big holes in chiffon cakes. When Dutch-processed cocoa powder is used, only baking powder is required.

6

Salt

Only a pinch of salt is required in these chiffon cake recipes to help perk up the other flavours in the cake and also to offset the sweetness of the cake.

WET INGREDIENTS

7

Eggs

Medium eggs weighing on average 60 g (with shell) are used in all the recipes in this book.

Chiffon cakes require the egg yolks and egg whites to be separated. Cold eggs separate more easily, but eggs whip to a higher volume when at room temperature. If preferred, you can separate the eggs when cold, then set them aside for 10–15 minutes to warm to room temperature.

When separating the egg yolk from the egg white, use a separate bowl to avoid getting any egg yolk in the lot of egg whites should the egg yolk break. The presence of egg yolk may affect the foaming properties of the egg white.

Egg whites from fresh eggs (less than 4 days old) are important for whipping up beautiful and stable meringues for chiffon cakes. Egg whites from older eggs are thinner and form less stable meringues as the liquid can separate more easily. Storing the eggs in a cool place will help to keep them fresh for longer.

8 Oil

I use vegetable, corn or coconut oil, but any light or mild tasting vegetable oil is suitable for use in these recipes. Oil is used in chiffon cakes to give the cakes a lighter, more airy texture compared to cakes made using butter. In our experience, there are no significant differences in taste and texture from using vegetable or corn oil.

9 Liquid (Water, Fruit Purée, Juice, Milk, Coconut Milk, Yoghurt, Tea or Cream Cheese)

The liquid content of chiffon cakes is typically made up of ingredients such as water, fruit purées, juices, milk, yoghurt, tea or cream cheese in addition to oil. As a higher liquid to flour ratio will yield a softer albeit less stable chiffon cake, we have optimised the ratio in these recipes to obtain the softest texture possible. Thus, it is essential that the measurements are taken accurately to ensure the cake turns out successfully.

10 Extract and Flavouring

Extracts and flavourings such as vanilla extract, strawberry paste and pandan paste and peppermint extract etc. are used in small amounts in these recipes to enhance the flavour of the cake. They are typically packaged in small bottles and are available from baking supply stores as well as some supermarkets.

Zest from citrus fruit such as mandarin oranges and lemons is used in some recipes to flavour the cakes. The zest is obtained by grating the thin, coloured outer layer of the citrus fruit. Avoid grating the white layer under the zest as it is bitter. Like extracts and flavourings, zest helps to enhance flavour and taste in baking.

11 Food Colouring

Although artificial/synthetic food colouring will produce more vibrant colours in baking, I try to use natural colouring as much as possible. Examples of natural colouring options include dry powders such as cocoa powder, charcoal powder, red yeast powder and matcha powder, as well as extracts such as blue pea flower extract, red roselle extract and yellow gardenia extract. To obtain a naturally white or lighter chiffon cakes, I reduce the number of egg yolks in the recipe or add cream cheese.

Basic Recipes & Techniques

Chiffon cake step-by-step guide

Egg yolk batter

Egg yolks
Castor sugar
Vegetable/corn oil
Water/fruit purée/juice/milk/yoghurt
Vanilla extract/flavouring
Cake flour, sifted
Cocoa powder, sifted
Baking powder, sifted
Salt

Meringue

Egg whites
Cream of tartar
Castor sugar

1. Prepare egg yolk batter. Using an electric mixer at medium speed, beat egg yolks and sugar in a mixing bowl until pale in colour.
2. Add oil, water/fruit purée/juice/milk/yoghurt and vanilla extract/flavouring. Mix well and set aside.
3. In another bowl, sift together any powdered ingredients such as flour, cocoa powder and baking powder.
4. Add sifted ingredients and salt to egg yolk batter. Mix until no trace of flour is found. Set aside.
5. Prepare meringue. In a clean, grease-free mixing bowl, whisk egg whites with cream of tartar at high speed until foamy.
6. Add half the sugar and whisk at high speed until soft peaks form.
7. Add remaining sugar and continue to whisk at high speed until firm peaks form.
8. Using a spatula, gently fold meringue into egg yolk batter one-third at a time.
9. Pour batter into desired mould. If baking in a baking pan, level batter with a pastry scraper. Gently tap mould on counter top to release any air bubbles.
10. Bake as instructed in recipe until top of cake springs back slightly when lightly pressed with a finger and a skewer inserted into the centre of cake comes out clean. Remove from oven.
11. If cake is baked in a tube pan, invert pan on a wire rack once out of the oven and set aside to cool completely before unmoulding. This is to ensure that the delicate cake does not collapse on its own weight while cooling. Cooling may take up to 2 hours.
12. Some bakers prefer to shock the cake by dropping it still in the pan, when it is fresh out of the oven, from a height of about 10 cm, before leaving to cool upright. This shock treatment is thought to prevent shrinkage.

1

2

4

5

6

7

8

9

Basic chiffon cake recipe

Makes one 18-cm round cake

Egg yolk batter

3 egg yolks

20 g castor sugar

39 g vegetable/corn oil

48 g orange juice

Zest from 1$^1/_2$ oranges

60 g cake flour, sifted

A pinch of salt

Meringue

4 egg whites

$^1/_4$ tsp cream of tartar

45 g castor sugar

1. Preheat oven to 160°C. Prepare an 18-cm round chiffon tube pan.
2. Prepare egg yolk batter (page 20) and meringue (page 20). Gently fold meringue into egg yolk batter one-third at a time.
3. Pour batter into chiffon tube pan until batter is 2 cm from rim of pan. Gently tap pan on counter top to release any air bubbles.
4. Bake at 160°C for 15 minutes, then 140°C for 30 minutes, or until a skewer inserted into the centre of cake comes out clean.
5. Invert pan on a wire rack and let cool completely before unmoulding.

Test with a skewer

Invert pan on an elevated wire rack

Unmoulding chiffon cakes from tube pans

1. To unmould, gently pull cake from sides of tube pan, turning tube pan as you go to loosen sides of cake.
2. Lift removable base up to unmould sides.
3. Gently lift cake from base using one hand, turning cake as you go, to loosen base of cake.
4. Invert cake. Lift and remove base of tube pan to release cake.

Scan the QR code to view a video tutorial on unmoulding chiffon cakes from tube pans.

Unmoulding chiffon cakes from glass or metal moulds, paper cones and eggshells

Glass or Metal Mould: Pull cake away from sides of mould to loosen cake, then invert mould to release cake.

Paper Cone: Unmould by peeling paper cone from narrow end, following sealed edge of paper cone to ensure tip of cake does not break off.

Eggshell: Unmould by gently cracking the eggshell all around the cake using the back of a metal spoon, then peeling off the shell in small pieces.

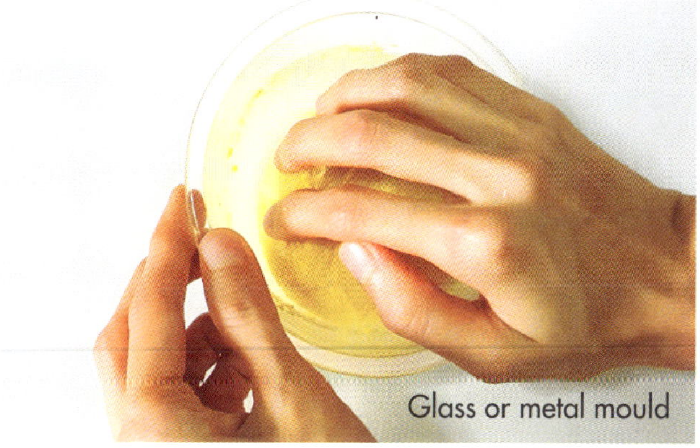

Glass or metal mould

Paper cone

Eggshell

Unmoulding chiffon cakes from paper cupcake cases, silicone moulds and silicone Bundts

Waxed Cupcake Case: Pull apart folds of cupcake case and invert to release cake.

Silicone Mould: Pull cake away from sides of mould to loosen cake, then invert mould and push outwards to release cake.

Silicone Bundt: Starting from outer ring of mould, pull cake away from sides of mould to loosen cake all round, before repeating step with inner ring. Place a cake board over mould and invert mould, then pull mould outwards to release cake. Shake mould to help release cake if needed.

Paper cupcake case

Silicone mould

Silicone Bundt

Making marshmallow cream

1. To adhere cake to cake, marshmallow cream is used.
2. To make, place 3–4 white marshmallows in a microwave-safe bowl and sprinkle with a little water. Heat in the microwave oven on High for 30 seconds, then remove and stir until smooth.
3. If mixture is too dry, add a few drops of hot water and stir. If too watery, add 1–2 marshmallows and repeat heating process.
4. Alternatively, melt marshmallows with a sprinkle of water in a double boiler and stir.

Making syrup

1. Small parts of the cake can be kept moist by brushing with syrup.
2. Syrup can be made in a 1:2 ratio or 1:3 ratio of sugar to water depending on how sweet or thick you prefer it to be.
3. Dissolve 10 g sugar in 20–30 g hot water. Stir well and set aside to cool.

Natural Food Colouring Guide

Cakes can be naturally coloured using a variety of ingredients such as strawberry purée, roselle flower juice, pumpkin purée, blueberry powder, blue pea flower juice, pandan juice, charcoal powder and cocoa powder among others, but the colours may not be as vivid as using food colouring. Here are some suggestions on natural sources of food colouring.

Green colouring from pandan leaves

1. Pandan juice will add a light fragrance and green tinge to cakes.
2. Prepare fresh pandan juice by blending 10–15 fresh pandan leaves (tips trimmed and cut into small pieces) with 50 g water.
3. Strain with a sieve and extract all the liquid. Discard pulp.

Blue colouring from dried pea flowers

1. To make a natural blue colouring, place about 35 dried blue pea flowers in a small bowl with 10 g hot water. Ensure flowers are fully submerged.
2. Let soak for 15–30 minutes, then strain liquid into another bowl, squeezing flowers to extract all the liquid. Discard pulp.

Red colouring from roselle flowers

1. To make a natural red colouring, place about 10 dried roselle flowers in a small bowl with 40 g hot water. Ensure flowers are fully submerged.
2. Sit bowl over a small pan of boiling water to create a bain-marie and let boil for 10 minutes. Alternatively, let flowers soak for 15–30 minutes, pressing flowers to extract the colour when they soften.
3. Strain liquid into another bowl, squeezing flowers to extract all the liquid. Discard pulp.

Yellow colouring from gardenia fruit

1. To make a natural yellow colouring, place about 10 dried gardenia fruit in a small bowl with 40 g hot water. Ensure fruit are fully submerged.
2. Let soak for 15–30 minutes, then strain liquid into another bowl. The fruit can be reboiled to extract more colouring if needed.

Chiffon Cake 101

Work quickly in a cool place

Meringue deflates quickly due to heat and humidity, so it is important to work quickly once the meringue is whipped. If possible, do not leave the meringue sitting around beyond 8–10 minutes, otherwise the cake may have many holes or a dense layer at the base from the separated meringue.

Ensure quality of meringue

The quality of the meringue is extremely important in ensuring that the resulting chiffon cake is soft and fluffy, and does not collapse upon cooling.

An under beaten meringue (soft peaks) will result in a very dense cake and an over beaten meringue (overly stiff and dry peaks) will cause the cake to crack openor explode its top, and also have a texture that is not as fine nor tender.

The perfect meringue should have firm peaks or just reach stiff peaks (but not beyond) and stick to the bowl when you overturn the bowl.

Make sure the bowl you use to beat the meringue is free of grease and dry. Do not use plastic bowls.

Use light and gentle strokes

Add the meringue to the egg yolk batter in 3 additions. Usually one-third of the meringue is folded into the egg yolk batter first to lighten the batter. Fold gently and lightly in the same direction, rotating the bowl as you go along. Do not over fold as over folding will cause the baked cake to have a very dense texture.

Use fresh eggs

A perfect meringue is the result not only of applying the correct technique of beating, but also of using fresh eggs. Store eggs in a cool, dry place to maximise shelf life.

Bake on the lowest rack

Chiffon cakes are typically baked on the lowest rack in the oven to prevent the top from cracking and browning too quickly. This will also prevent the chiffon cake from rising or expanding too quickly at the beginning which may cause the cake to contract and shrink later on.

Prevent drying out

Always keep chiffon cakes well wrapped up or in airtight containers to prevent them from drying out. Brush syrup on any small parts if you are not going to use them right away.

Cool in a place with good air circulation

Chiffon cakes baked in tube pans or large moulds need to be inverted while cooling to prevent the cake from collapsing from its own weight during the sensitive stage of cooling before the structure stabilises. For this, the cooling rack should be elevated to ensure there is air circulation underneath the cake and condensation will not form on the cake. You can also blast a fan at the cake to help cooling and improve the air circulation.

Special temperature control to reduce browning

For deco chiffon cakes, temperature control is important to prevention the formation of a brown crust that will hide the colour and pattern. The baking temperature is reduced from 160°C to 140°C or lower after 15 minutes of baking to prevent browning. The oven's fan mode is usually not used as this would raise the oven temperature and make the oven too hot. An oven thermometer is useful to help monitor the oven temperature. Steam baking will also help to control the oven temperature from rising too fast, and above the set temperature.

Baking temperature and timing

The optimal baking temperatures and timings are listed in the recipes, but as individual oven temperatures and conditions vary, it is best to use an oven thermometer to check the temperature of your oven and use a skewer to test the baked cakes for doneness.

Storing chiffon cakes

Stored in airtight containers, chiffon cakes will keep for up to 2 days at room temperature or up to 5 days refrigerated.

Troubleshooting Guide

General

Cake falls out of pan

Chiffon cake falls out of the pan when it is inverted for cooling and starts to shrink.

The chiffon cake is likely to be under baked. Try increasing the baking time by intervals of 5 minutes.

Cake shrinks

Chiffon cake shrinks after it is unmoulded.

The cake may not have been fully cooled before it was removed from the mould and hence its structure would not have been completely stabilised, causing it to shrink. Unmould the cake only after it is fully cool.

Cake has exploded top

Chiffon cake has an overly exploded top causing the cake to have a wide base when inverted.

The meringue may have been over beaten and too stiff, or the chiffon tube pan was filled too full. The perfect meringue should be firm and glossy. When filling the chiffon tube pan, leave a minimum 2 cm gap from the rim of the pan.

Cake forms a waist

Chiffon cake forms a waist upon cooling.

The chiffon cake is likely to be under baked. Try increasing the baking time by intervals of 5 minutes.

Cake has large air pockets

Chiffon cake has large air pockets.

Before placing the pan into the oven to bake, tap it gently on the counter top to release any air bubbles. If the air pockets are uneven and there are specks of white in the pockets, the meringue may not have been folded in completely or uniformly.

Cake is dry

Chiffon cake is dry.

The chiffon cake is likely to be overbaked. Try reducing the baking time by intervals of 5–10 minutes.

Cake is sticky on top

Chiffon cake is moist or has a sticky top layer when it is taken out of the oven.

The chiffon cake is likely under baked. Return it to the oven to bake a few minutes longer until the top layer is dry.

Cake browns

Chiffon cake browns, hiding the colour/pattern.

Since individual ovens may work differently, try reducing the temperature of the oven by 10°C each time until you get the optimum temperature for baking these coloured chiffon cakes in your oven.

Cake cracks

Chiffon cake has cracks on top once it is taken out of the oven.

Fret not! Small cracks are normal and will not be seen once the cake is inverted. If the cracks are large, you may have overfilled the mould. When filling a mould with batter, leave a minimum 2 cm gap from the rim of the mould. If preferred, steam baking may help to eliminate cracks. To steam bake, place a pan of water under the lowest rack in the oven to create steam while the cake bakes.

Cake does not rise

Chiffon cake does not rise.

The meringue was likely under whipped or overfolded, or the baking pan was greased. Ensure to whip the meringue to firm peaks. When folding the meringue into the egg yolk batter, fold gently in circular, unidirectional strokes, just up to the point of uniform incorporation. Do not grease the baking pan.

Cake caves in

Top of the chiffon cake caves in after it is cooled and removed from the mould.

The liquid to flour ratio was wrong, causing the cake to be heavy and pulled down while it was inverted. Ensure that all ingredients are measured correctly and accurately. Do not use baking paper to line the base of the pan. If the pan is lined, the cake will not be able to cling to the pan to help it rise. As a result, the top of the cake will be sunken and wrinkled after cooling.

Cake sticks to mould

Chiffon cake sticks to the mould and cannot be removed without tearing.

This could be due to several reasons: the cake is under baked, it was unmoulded when it was not completely cooled or it does not have enough oil content (double check the amount of oil used). You can try to salvage the cake by using a spatula or cake knife to loosen the portion stuck to the pan while using your hand to unmould or peel off the rest of the cake.

To avoid this happening again, let the cake bake a few minutes longer, ensure it is fully cooled before unmoulding and check that the amount of oil has been measured correctly.

Cake forms a dense layer

Cake forms a dense layer at the base.

The meringue likely broke down at the base due to the long working time or because the batter was overfolded. When folding the meringue into the egg yolk batter, fold gently in circular, unidirectional strokes, just up to the point of uniform incorporation. Work quickly to fold in the meringue after it has been whipped.

Another reason for this is that the oven is not uniformly heated at the top and bottom.

Cake forms a sticky layer

Chiffon cake forms a moist or sticky layer after cooling or after a few hours or a day, although it was dry when it was first taken out of the oven.

This is normal as chiffon cakes tend to absorb moisture over time when the air is humid. This is due to the sugar content in the cake and will vary with the recipe. Let the sticky layer dry up by leaving it exposed or remove it by gently placing a piece of baking paper over the layer and then removing it. The sticky layer will peel off with the baking paper.

Cake dries during assembly

Chiffon cakes, especially the small parts, dry up during assembly.

Remember to brush the cakes with syrup (page 27), especially any small parts when the assembly time is long. Always keep the cakes in an airtight container if not using/serving immediately or store them in the refrigerator.

Patterned Chiffon Cakes

Pattern sticks to mould

The pattern sticks to the mould and does not lift off with the cake when unmoulding.

The batter for the pattern was piped too thinly. It needs to be thicker, at least 5 mm thick, for it to be able to adhere to the cake after baking.

Pattern flakes or peels off

After the cake is unmoulded, the pattern flakes or peels off the cake.

The meringue for the pattern batter was likely too stiff and was not well incorporated, leading the pattern to flake or peel off the baked cake.

Holes between patterns and cake

The chiffon cake has holes between the patterns and cake.

You will need to be careful to fill up the gaps in between the patterns when piping the new layer of batter.

Pattern is disturbed

The pattern is disturbed when the second batter is added.

You need to be gentle when adding the second layer of batter. Use a teaspoon and add the batter over the first layer lightly.

Pattern sunk

The pattern sunk into the cake while baking.

This can happen with cakes where the pattern is baked, then cut out and arranged in the mould before it is baked again. Ensure that the cut-outs are kept moist in an airtight container and arrange them with the moist surface facing the base of the mould only when the batter is ready.

Pattern has holes

The pattern has holes.

This could be due to the breaking down of the meringue in the pattern batter, either because of the prolonged piping (heat from hands deflated the batter) or the pattern was under baked and the form was not stabilised.

Multicoloured Chiffon Cakes

Colours are messed up

When the multicoloured chiffon cake is unmoulded, the colour at the top of the cake is from another layer and not what it should be.

The meringue in the base layer may have broken down due to the prolonged working time spooning in the batter. You will need to work faster after the batters have been folded. Have your equipment on hand and know the steps ahead of time.

The meringue may also have been under whipped such that the batters at the base layers were not viscous enough to support the upper layers. Whip the meringue to firmer peaks. A meringue at this stage will hold its shape when the whisk is turned upside down.

Batter flattens

When making a patterned chiffon cake (e.g. with waves or spots), the batter does not hold its shape and flattens.

The meringue is likely under whipped or overfolded such that the batter flows instead of holding its shape. Whipping the meringue to firm peaks and having the right folding technique is important when making patterned chiffon cakes.

Colours not distinct

When the multicoloured chiffon cake is umoulded, the different layers are not distinct but mixed up.

The meringue is likely to be under whipped or overfolded such that the batters at the base layers were not viscous enough to support the upper layers. The meringue will need to be whipped up to firmer peaks. The folding action needs to be gentle and in circular, unidirectional strokes, just up to the point of uniform incorporation.

Layers not flat

When making striped or rainbow chiffon cakes, the layers do not turn out flat.

The meringue may have been too stiff, such that it was difficult to spread the batter smoothly into an even layer. Another reason may be that too much force was used to spread the batter causing the layers below to be disturbed. Ensure that the meringue is whipped to firm peaks and is not overly stiff. Use light and gentle strokes to spread the batter evenly over the previous layer without disturbing the layers below.

All Creatures Great & Small

Charcoal-Vanilla Koala Cupcakes

Makes three 11-cm cupcakes

Egg yolk batter

3 egg yolks

20 g castor sugar

39 g vegetable/corn oil

42 g water

1 tsp vanilla extract

60 g cake flour, sifted

1 tsp charcoal powder, sifted

Pink gel food colouring

A pinch of baking powder, sifted

Meringue

4 egg whites

$^{1}/_{4}$ tsp cream of tartar

45 g castor sugar

Finishing

Marshmallow cream (page 27)

1. Preheat oven to 160°C. Prepare three 11-cm round glass bowls, a silicone cake pop mould with 3-cm cavities and another with 5-cm cavities. Line a 15-cm square baking pan with baking paper.
2. Prepare egg yolk batter (page 20). Spoon 10 tsp batter into a small bowl and add $^{3}/_{4}$ tsp charcoal powder. Mix well for black batter. Spoon 5 tsp batter into a second bowl and add little pink gel food colouring. Mix well for pink batter. To remaining batter, add $^{1}/_{4}$ tsp charcoal powder and baking powder. Mix well for grey batter.
3. Prepare meringue (page 20). Gently fold meringue into each batter one-third at a time: 20 Tbsp meringue into black batter, 10 Tbsp meringue into pink batter, and remaining meringue into grey batter.
4. Spoon black batter into three 3-cm cavities in cake pop mould for noses. Spoon grey batter into six 5-cm cavities in cake pop mould for outer ears. Cake pop cavities should be filled 80–90% full. Divide remaining grey batter among 3 glass bowls for faces. Gently tap moulds on counter top to release any air bubbles.
5. Bake black cake pops at 160°C for 12 minutes and grey cake pops for 15 minutes. Bake cake in bowls at 160°C for 15 minutes, then 150°C for 15 minutes or until a skewer inserted into the centre of cakes comes out clean. Invert bowls on a wire rack to cool completely before unmoulding. Silicone moulds can be cooled upright.
6. Pour remaining black batter and pink batter side by side into prepared baking pan. Gently tap pan on counter top to release any air bubbles. Bake at 160°C for 15 minutes. Invert sheet cake onto a sheet of baking paper and let cool.
7. Peel baking paper from sheet cake and place on a cutting mat. Use a small round cutter to cut koala's mouth from black sheet cake. Do this by cutting a circle and then making another circular cut 1 mm away. Use a small round cutter to cut 6 small circles from black sheet cake for eyes. Use a 3-cm round cutter to cut 6 circles from pink sheet cake for inner ears.
8. Gently shape black cake pops into ovals for noses. Assemble parts using marshmallow cream.

Cream Cheese Panda Cakes

Makes one 13-cm and one 20-cm oval cake

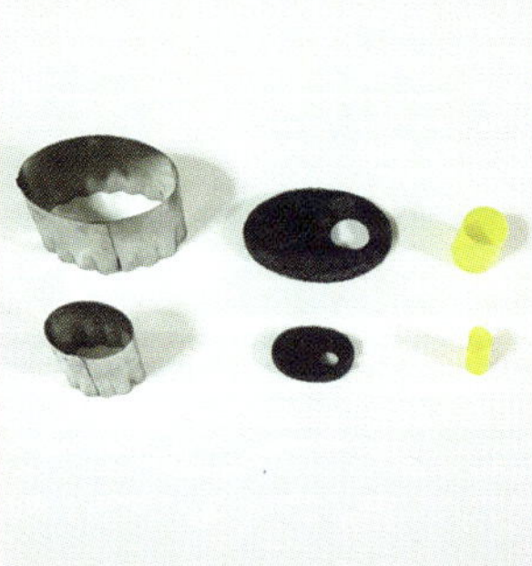

Egg yolk batter

167 g milk

167 g cream cheese, cut into small cubes

3 egg yolks

58 g castor sugar

67 g vegetable/coconut oil

133 g cake flour, sifted

$^{1}/_{4}$ tsp salt, sifted

$1^{1}/_{2}$ tsp charcoal powder, sifted

$^{1}/_{4}$ tsp baking powder, sifted

Meringue

7 egg whites

$^{1}/_{4}$ tsp cream of tartar

47 g castor sugar

Finishing

Marshmallow cream (page 27)

1. Warm milk using a hot water bath. Add cream cheese and stir until completely dissolved and no lumps are left. Set aside to cool before using in egg yolk batter.
2. Preheat oven to 160°C. Prepare 2 oval glass bowls, 13-cm x 10-cm and 20-cm x 14-cm, and a silicone cake pop mould with 3-cm cavities. Line a 15-cm square baking pan with baking paper.
3. Prepare egg yolk batter (page 20). Spoon 20 tsp batter into a small bowl and add charcoal powder and baking powder. Mix well for black batter. Leave remaining batter plain.
4. Prepare meringue (page 20). Gently fold meringue into each batter in 2 additions: 40 Tbsp ($2^{1}/_{2}$ cups) meringue into black batter and remaining meringue into plain batter.
5. Spoon some black batter into a piping bag and cut a 2-mm hole at the tip. Pipe a 2-cm thick black arc in each bowl. Bake at 160°C for 2 minutes.
6. Pour plain batter over baked black arcs in glass bowls until bowls are two-thirds full. Bake smaller bowl at 160°C for 15 minutes, 150°C for 10 minutes and 140°C for 10 minutes. Bake bigger bowl at 160°C for 15 minutes, 150°C for 10 minutes and 140°C for 20–25 minutes. A skewer inserted into the centre of cakes should come out clean. Invert bowls on a wire rack to cool completely before unmoulding.
7. Spoon some black batter into 6 cake pop cavities: fill 3 cake pop cavities until full (for big panda) and another 3 cake pop cavities until two-thirds full (for small panda). Pour remaining black batter into prepared baking pan and gently tap pan on counter top to release any air bubbles. Bake cake pops at 160°C for 12 minutes and sheet cake for 15 minutes. Invert sheet cake onto a sheet of baking paper and let cool.
8. Peel baking paper from sheet cake and place on a cutting mat. Use round cutters to cut 2 large circles for big panda's ears and 2 small circles for small panda's ears. Trim to shape ears.
9. Use oval cutters to cut 2 large ovals for big panda's eyes and 2 small ovals for small panda's eyes. Punch out a small circle from each oval using small round cutters. Use a small round cutter to cut smiling eyes for big panda. Do this by cutting a circle and then making another circular cut 1 mm away.
10. Cut triangles for noses. Cut cake pops in half for feet and tails.
11. Assemble parts on cake using marshmallow cream. Use a pink food marker to add rosy cheeks.

Black Sesame-Adzuki Ladybird Chiffon Pops

Makes 8–10 cake pops

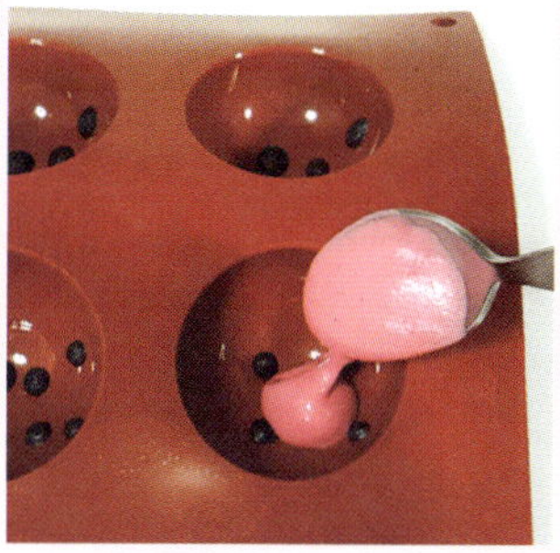
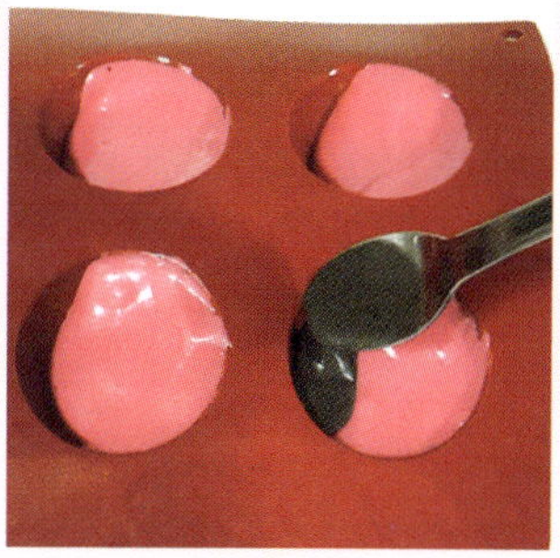

Egg yolk batter

2 egg yolks

12 g castor sugar

25 g vegetable/corn oil

26 g water

$^1/_2$ tsp vanilla extract

40 g cake flour, sifted

A pinch of salt

11 g black sesame paste

$^1/_4$ tsp charcoal powder or black gel food colouring

Baking powder, as needed, sifted

24 g smooth adzuki bean paste

$^1/_2$ tsp red yeast powder or a few drops of red food colouring

Meringue

3 egg whites

$^1/_4$ tsp cream of tartar

30 g castor sugar

Finishing

Marshmallow cream (page 27)

> *Note* If the piping batter is too runny, add another $^1/_3$ tsp cake flour until the batter holds its shape after piping.

1. Preheat oven to 160°C. Prepare a silicone cake pop mould with 5-cm cavities. Line a 15-cm square baking pan with baking paper.
2. Prepare egg yolk batter (page 20). Spoon 4 tsp batter into a small bowl and add black sesame paste, charcoal powder or black gel food colouring and a pinch of baking powder for black batter. Spoon 4 tsp batter into a second bowl and leave plain. Spoon 1 tsp batter into a third bowl and add $^1/_3$ tsp cake flour and $^1/_3$ tsp charcoal powder or black gel food colouring for piping batter. To remaining batter, add adzuki bean paste, $^1/_4$ tsp baking powder and red yeast powder or red food colouring for red batter. Mix well for all batters.
3. Prepare meringue (page 20). Gently fold meringue into each batter in 2 additions: 8 Tbsp meringue into black batter, 8 Tbsp meringue into plain batter, 2 Tbsp meringue into piping batter and remainder into red batter.
4. Spoon piping batter into a piping bag and cut a 2-mm hole at the tip. Pipe 6 small dots on the right hand side of each cavity in cake pop mould. Bake at 160°C for 2 minutes.
5. Spoon red batter gently over baked black dots in cake pop mould until three-quarters full. Fill remaining space on left hand side of cake pop cavities with black batter. Bake at 160°C for 15 minutes or until a skewer inserted into the centre of cakes comes out clean. Leave on a wire rack to cool completely before unmoulding.
6. Pour remaining black and plain batters side by side in prepared baking pan. Gently tap pan on counter top to release any air bubbles. Bake at 160°C for 15 minutes. Invert sheet cake onto a sheet of baking paper and let cool.
7. Use a knife to make a cut at the centre of each cake pop to create ladybird's wings.
8. Peel baking paper from sheet cake and place on a cutting mat. Use round cutters to cut 2 big white circles and 2 small black circles from white and black sheet cakes for eyes for each ladybird. You can also use liquorice lace candy for the eyes. Assemble parts using marshmallow cream.

Yoghurt Sheep Chiffon Pops

Makes 14 cake pops

Egg yolk batter

1 egg yolk

13 g castor sugar

26 g vegetable/corn oil

33 g plain yoghurt drink

$^{3}/_{4}$ tsp vanilla extract

40 g cake flour, sifted

$^{1}/_{3}$ tsp charcoal powder, sifted

Meringue

3 egg whites

$^{1}/_{4}$ tsp cream of tartar

30 g castor sugar

Finishing

Marshmallow cream (page 27)

Charcoal powder

1. Preheat oven to 160°C. Prepare a silicone cake pop mould with 3-cm cavities. Line an 18-cm square baking pan with baking paper.
2. Prepare egg yolk batter (page 20). Spoon 6 tsp batter into a small bowl and add charcoal powder. Mix well for black batter. Leave remaining batter plain.
3. Prepare meringue (page 20). Gently fold meringue into each batter one-third at a time: 12 Tbsp meringue into black batter and remainder into plain batter.
4. Spoon plain batter into 14 cavities in cake pop mould until 80–90% full. Bake at 160°C for 12 minutes or until a skewer inserted into the centre of cakes comes out clean. Leave on a wire rack to cool completely before unmoulding.
5. Pour black batter and remaining plain batter side by side in prepared baking pan. Gently tap pan on counter top to release any air bubbles. Bake at 160°C for 15 minutes. Invert sheet cake onto a sheet of baking paper and let cool.
6. Place cake pops on a cutting mat and use a small round fluted edge cutter to cut shape of sheep.
7. Peel baking paper from sheet cake and place on a cutting mat. For each sheep, use oval cutters to cut an oval for the face and 2 small ovals for the ears from black sheet cake. Use a small straw to cut 2 circles for the eyes from plain sheet cake.
8. Assemble parts using marshmallow cream.
9. Using a toothpick, draw eyeballs on sheep's eyes using charcoal powder. Using a clean toothpick, make 2 holes for the nose.

Banana-Pandan Dinosaur Cupcakes

Makes 12 cupcakes

Recipe on pages 50 and 51

Banana chiffon cupcakes

Egg yolk batter

1 egg yolk

7 g castor sugar

21 g vegetable/corn/coconut oil

47 g cake flour, sifted

$^{1}/_{5}$ tsp baking soda, sifted

$^{1}/_{5}$ tsp baking powder, sifted

$^{1}/_{5}$ tsp salt, sifted

94 g banana purée (using 2 large ripe bananas)

Meringue

2 egg whites

$^{1}/_{4}$ tsp cream of tartar

23 g castor sugar

Pandan sheet cake

Egg yolk batter

2 egg yolks

13 g castor sugar

26 g vegetable/corn/coconut oil

17 g coconut milk

10 g pandan juice (page 28)

$^{1}/_{3}$ tsp vanilla extract

$^{2}/_{3}$ tsp pandan paste

40 g cake flour, sifted

A pinch of salt

Meringue

3 egg whites

$^{1}/_{4}$ tsp cream of tartar

30 g castor sugar

1. Preheat oven to 160°C. Prepare 12 waxed cupcake cases, each 3.5 cm wide. Line 3 square baking pans with baking paper: 25-cm, 23-cm and 15-cm. Prepare a silicone dinosaur cake pop mould.

2. Prepare egg yolk batter (page 20) and meringue (page 20) for banana chiffon cupcakes. Gently fold meringue into egg yolk batter one-third at a time. Fill cupcake cases until batter is about 1 cm from rim of cases.

3. Bake banana chiffon cupcakes at 160°C for 10 minutes, then 150°C for 15 minutes, or until a skewer inserted into the centre of cakes comes out clean. Let cool.

4. Prepare egg yolk batter (page 20) and meringue (page 20) for pandan sheet cake. Gently fold meringue into egg yolk batter one-third at a time. Pour pandan batter into prepared 25-cm and 23-cm pans. Gently tap pans on counter top to release any air bubbles.

5. Bake at 160°C for 15 minutes. Invert each sheet cake onto a sheet of baking paper and let cool.

Dinosaur chiffon pops

Egg yolk batter

1 egg yolk

10 g castor sugar

21 g vegetable/corn oil

22 g water

3 g vanilla extract

30 g cake flour, sifted

Red, yellow, orange and brown gel food colouring or natural colouring (red: roselle extract, yellow: gardenia yellow extract, orange: mixture of roselle extract and gardenia yellow extract, brown: cocoa powder)

Meringue

2 egg whites

$^{1}/_{8}$ tsp cream of tartar

23 g castor sugar

Finishing

Marshmallow cream (page 27)

Charcoal powder

6. Prepare egg yolk batter (page 20) for dinosaur chiffon pops. Spoon batter equally into 5 small bowls. Add a different food colouring to 4 bowls and mix well. Leave one portion plain.
7. Prepare meringue (page 20) for dinosaur chiffon pops. Divide meringue into 5 equal portions. Gently and quickly fold meringue into each egg yolk batter one-third at a time.
8. Spoon each coloured batter into 3 cavities in dinosaur cake pop mould to fill a total of 12 cavities. Bake at 160°C for 12 minutes or until a skewer inserted into the centre of cakes comes out clean. Leave on a wire rack to cool completely before unmoulding.
9. Pour remaining plain batter into prepared 15-cm baking pan. Bake at 160°C for 15 minutes. Invert sheet cake onto a sheet of baking paper and let cool.
10. Peel baking paper from sheet cakes and place on a cutting mat. Use a 6-cm round cutter to cut out 12 green circles from pandan sheet cakes. Place one on each cupcake and keep in place using marshmallow cream.
11. Using small round cutters and a knife, cut circles and strips from leftover pandan sheet cake for pattern on dinosaurs. Using a small straw, cut out 24 circles from plain sheet cake for dinosaur's eyes.
12. Assemble parts using marshmallow cream. Using a toothpick, draw eyeballs on dinosaur's eyes using charcoal powder.

Matcha Turtle Sea Waves Cake

Makes one 23-cm cake

Recipe on pages 54 and 55

Sea waves chiffon

Egg yolk batter

6 egg yolks

53 g castor sugar

105 g vegetable/corn oil

107 g milk

13 g vanilla extract

160 g cake flour, sifted

2 tsp blue pea flower extract (page 28)

Blue gel food colouring (optional)

Meringue

11 egg whites

1/2 tsp cream of tartar

120 g castor sugar

Matcha chiffon

Egg yolk batter

1 egg yolk

7 g castor sugar

13 g vegetable/corn oil

20 g cake flour, sifted

A pinch of salt

Dark green matcha tea: 1 1/4 tsp matcha powder in 10 g hot milk

Light green matcha tea: 1/4 tsp matcha powder in 10 g hot milk

Meringue

1 1/2 egg whites

1/4 tsp cream of tartar

15 g castor sugar

> *Note* Dissolving the matcha powder in hot milk prevents the cake from having uneven specks of green powder.

1. Preheat oven to 160°C. Prepare a 23-cm chiffon tube pan.
2. Prepare egg yolk batter (page 20) for sea waves chiffon. Divide batter equally into 2 portions. To one portion, add blue pea flower extract and a little blue gel food colouring to brighten the colour if desired. Mix well for a light blue batter. Leave other portion plain.
3. Prepare meringue (page 20) for sea waves chiffon. Divide meringue equally into 2 portions and gently fold each portion into light blue and plain batters one-third at a time.
4. Pour some plain batter into chiffon cube pan to create a base layer about 2 cm thick. With remaining plain batter, create mounds by dropping spoonfuls of batter at intervals, close to sides of pan. Smoothen edge of mounds using a chopstick.
5. Spoon blue batter to fill spaces between mounds, until batter is about 2 cm from rim of pan. Gently tap pan on counter top to release any bubbles.
6. Bake at 160°C for 15 minutes, 150°C for 10 minutes, 140°C for 20 minutes, then 130°C for 15 minutes, or until a skewer inserted into the centre of cake comes out clean.
7. Invert pan on a wire rack to cool completely before unmoulding.
8. Prepare an egg shell as a mould for turtle head. Make a hole using a chopsticks on the side of egg (refer to image of egg shell on page 10). Drain egg, rinse and remove membrane. Leave to air-dry. Place egg shell in a waxed cupcake case to hold shell in place.
9. Prepare a 10-cm x 13-cm oval glass bowl. Line an 18-cm square baking pan with baking paper.
10. Preheat oven to 160°C.
11. Prepare egg yolk batter (page 20). Divide batter equally into 2 portions. Add 8 g dark green matcha tea to one portion and 8 g light green matcha tea to the other portion. Mix well for dark and light green batters.
12. Prepare meringue (page 20). Divide meringue into 2 equal portions and gently fold meringue one-third at a time into dark and light green batters.
13. Spoon one-third of light green batter into a piping bag and cut a 2-mm hole at the tip. Pipe hexagons on base of oval glass bowl. Bake at 160°C for 2 minutes. Set bowl aside to cool.

Turtle eyes chiffon

Egg yolk batter

1 egg yolk

7 g castor sugar

13 g vegetable/corn oil

19 g water

20 g cake flour

Black gel food colouring or $^3/_4$ tsp charcoal powder

Meringue

$1^1/_2$ egg whites

$^1/_4$ tsp cream of tartar

15 g castor sugar

Finishing

Marshmallow cream (page 27)

14. When bowl is cool, spoon dark green batter over baked hexagons until bowl is half to two-thirds full. Bake at 160°C for 15 minutes, then 150°C for 15–20 minutes, or until a skewer inserted into the centre of cake comes out clean.
15. Invert bowl on a wire rack to cool completely before unmoulding.
16. Spoon light green batter into prepared eggshell until two-thirds full, then pour remaining batter into baking pan. Tap moulds gently on counter top to release any air bubbles.
17. Bake eggshell at 160°C for 15 minutes, then 150°C for 5–10 minutes. Bake sheet cake at 160°C for 15 minutes. Place eggshell on a wire rack to cool completely before unmoulding. Invert sheet cake on a sheet of baking paper and let cool.
18. Preheat oven to 160°C. Prepare a silicone cake pop mould with 3-cm cavities. Line a 15-cm square baking pan with baking paper.
19. Prepare egg yolk batter (page 20) for turtle eyes chiffon. Spoon 2 tsp batter into a small bowl for plain batter. Add black gel food colouring or charcoal powder to remaining batter and mix well.
20. Prepare meringue (page 20) for turtle eyes chiffon. Gently fold meringue into each batter one-third at a time: 4 Tbsp meringue into plain batter and remainder into black batter.
21. Fill 2 cake pop cavities with plain batter until one-third or half full. Bake at 160°C for 11–12 minutes. Leave on a wire rack to cool completely before unmoulding.
22. Pour remaining plain and black batters side by side into baking pan. Gently tap pan on counter top to release any air bubbles. Bake at 160°C for 15 minutes. Invert sheet cake onto a sheet of baking paper and let cool.
23. Fill centre of tube cake with a hidden surprise. Brush top surface of cake with marshmallow cream and place oval turtle cake over to conceal surprise. Place egg shell cake in front of oval cake for turtle head. Assemble using marshmallow cream.
24. Peel baking paper from sheet cake and place on a cutting mat. Use a large round cutter to cut eye balls from black sheet cake. Use a small round cutter to cut small circles for glint in eyes from white sheet cake. Assemble using marshmallow cream.
25. Peel baking paper from light green sheet cake and place on a cutting mat. Use an oval cutter to cut an oval from sheet cake, then make another cut 1.5 cm away to create turtle's flippers. Cut 4 of these. Assemble using marshmallow cream.

Vanilla-Pandan Rabbit-in-Burrow Cake

Makes one 18-cm cake

Recipe on pages 58 and 59

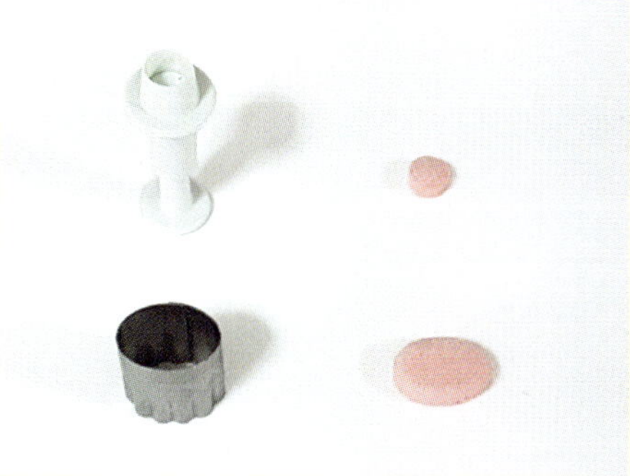

Pandan chiffon

Egg yolk batter

3 egg yolks

20 g castor sugar

39 g vegetable/corn/coconut oil

25 g coconut milk

15 g pandan juice (page 28)

1/2 tsp vanilla extract

1 tsp pandan paste

60 g cake flour, sifted

A pinch of salt

Meringue

4 egg whites

1/4 tsp cream of tartar

45 g castor sugar

1. Preheat oven to 160°C. Prepare an 18-cm chiffon tube pan.
2. Prepare egg yolk batter (page 20) and meringue (page 20) for pandan chiffon. Gently fold meringue into egg yolk batter one-third at a time.
3. Pour pandan batter into chiffon tube pan until batter is 2 cm from rim of pan. Gently tap pan on counter top to release any air bubbles.
4. Bake at 160°C for 15 minutes, then 140°C for 30–31 minutes, or until a skewer inserted into the centre of cake comes out clean. Invert pan on a wire rack to cool completely before unmoulding.

Vanilla chiffon

Egg yolk batter

1 egg yolk

10 g castor sugar

19 g vegetable/corn oil

21 g water

1/2 tsp vanilla extract

26 g cake flour, sifted

Pink gel food colouring

Meringue

2 egg whites

1/4 tsp cream of tartar

22 g castor sugar

Finishing

Marshmallow cream (page 27)

5. Prepare an 11-cm round glass bowl and a cake pop mould with 3-cm cavities. Line a 15-cm square baking pan with baking paper. Preheat oven to 160°C.
6. Prepare egg yolk batter (page 20) for vanilla chiffon. Spoon 7 tsp batter into a small bowl and add pink food colouring. Mix well. Leave remaining batter plain.
7. Prepare meringue (page 20) for vanilla chiffon. Gently fold meringue into each batter one-third at a time: 14 Tbsp meringue into pink batter and remainder into plain batter.
8. Spoon plain batter into prepared 11-cm bowl and 3 cake pop cavities. Bake bowl at 160°C for 15 minutes, then 140°C for 15 minutes. Bake cake pops at 160°C for 12 minutes. Invert bowl and leave cake pop mould upright on wire rack to cool completely before unmoulding.
9. Pour pink batter into 15-cm baking pan. Bake at 160°C for 15 minutes. Invert sheet cake onto a sheet of baking paper and let cool.
10. Fill centre of tube cake with marshmallows or sweets for a hidden surprise. Brush a wide ring of cocoa powder around hole as soil. Brush some marshmallow cream on base of bowl cake and place it over hole to conceal surprise.
11. Brush a little marshmallow cream on a cake pop and position it on top of bowl cake for rabbit's tail. Shape 2 cake pops into ovals for rabbit's feet.
12. Peel baking paper from pink sheet cake and place on a cutting mat. Use oval and round cutters to cut out shapes for rabbit's feet. Assemble parts using marshmallow cream.
13. Decorate with icing flowers if desired.

Cream Cheese-Charcoal Moo Moo Cake

Makes one 20-cm cake

Cream cheese-charcoal chiffon

Egg yolk batter

200 g milk

200 g cream cheese, cut into small cubes

4 egg yolks

70 g castor sugar

80 g vegetable/corn/coconut oil

160 g cake flour, sifted

1/4 tsp salt, sifted

1 tsp charcoal powder, sifted

A pinch of baking powder

Meringue

8 egg whites

1/4 tsp cream of tartar

55 g castor sugar

Strawberry milk sheet cake

Egg yolk batter

1 egg yolk

7 g castor sugar

13 g vegetable/corn oil

19 g strawberry milk

20 g cake flour, sifted

Strawberry paste

Meringue

1 1/2 egg whites

1/4 tsp cream of tartar

15 g castor sugar

Finishing

Marshmallow cream (page 27)

1. Warm milk using a hot water bath. Add cream cheese and stir until completely dissolved and no lumps are left. Set aside to cool before using in egg yolk batter.
2. Preheat oven to 160°C. Prepare a 20-cm chiffon tube pan. Line a 15-cm square baking pan with baking paper.
3. Prepare egg yolk batter (page 20) for cream cheese-charcoal chiffon. Spoon 10 tsp batter into another bowl. Add charcoal powder and baking powder for black batter. Mix well.
4. Prepare meringue (page 20) for cream cheese-charcoal chiffon. Gently fold meringue into each batter one-third at a time: 20 Tbsp meringue into black batter and remainder into cream cheese batter.
5. Place spoonfuls of black batter into chiffon tube pan for patches on cow. Fill spaces among black batter with cream cheese batter. Repeat to make another layer. Top with remaining cream cheese batter until batter is 2 cm from rim of pan. Gently tap pan on counter top to release any air bubbles.
6. Bake at 160°C for 15 minutes, 150°C for 10 minutes, 140°C for 20 minutes and 130°C for 10–15 minutes, or until a skewer inserted into the centre of cake comes out clean. Invert pan on a wire rack to cool completely before unmoulding.
7. Preheat oven to 160°C. Pour remaining black batter into square baking pan. Bake at 160°C for 15 minutes. Invert sheet cake onto a sheet of baking paper and let cool.
8. Line a 20-cm square baking pan with baking paper.
9. Prepare egg yolk batter (page 20) and meringue (page 20) for strawberry sheet cake. Gently fold meringue into egg yolk batter one-third at a time.
10. Pour strawberry milk batter into baking pan. Bake at 160°C for 15 minutes. Invert sheet cake onto a sheet of baking paper and let cool.
11. Peel baking paper from sheet cakes and place on a cutting mat. From strawberry milk sheet cake: use oval cutters to cut a large oval for nose and small ovals for nostrils, and a heart-shape cutter to cut ears. From black sheet cake: use a teardrop-shape cutter to cut horns and a round cutter to cut smiling eyes. Do this by cutting a circle and then making another circular cut 1 mm away.
12. Assemble parts using marshmallow cream.

Around-the-World Vanilla-Pandan Cake

Makes one 23-cm cake

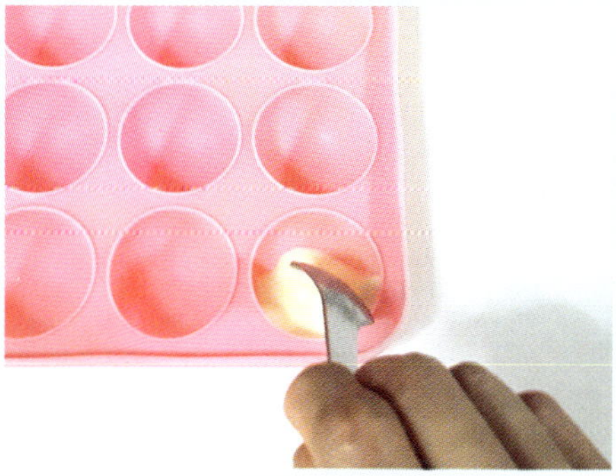

Recipe on pages 64 and 65

World chiffon

Egg yolk batter

8 egg yolks

53 g castor sugar

105 g vegetable/corn oil

101 g water

13 g vanilla extract

160 g cake flour, sifted

2 tsp blue pea flower extract (page 28)

Blue gel food colouring (optional)

1 tsp pandan paste

12 g coconut cream powder

Meringue

11 egg whites

1/2 tsp cream of tartar

120 g castor sugar

1. Preheat oven to 160°C. Prepare a 23-cm chiffon tube pan.
2. Prepare egg yolk batter (page 20) for world chiffon. Spoon two-thirds of batter into another bowl and add blue pea flower extract and a drop of blue gel food colouring, if desired, for blue batter. To remaining batter, add pandan paste and coconut cream powder for green batter.
3. Prepare meringue (page 20) for world chiffon. Gently fold meringue into each batter one-third at a time: two-thirds meringue into blue batter and remaining meringue into pandan batter.
4. Place spoonfuls of green batter into chiffon tube pan to create longish blobs for continents and use a chopstick to define shape if desired. Fill space among green batter with blue batter. Repeat to make another layer, then cover with remaining blue batter until batter is 2 cm from rim of pan. Gently tap pan on counter top to release any air bubbles.
5. Bake at 160°C for 15 minutes, 150°C for 10 minutes, 140°C for 20 minutes, and 130°C for 15 minutes, or until a skewer inserted into the centre of cake comes out clean. Invert pan on a wire rack to cool completely before unmoulding.

Boy-in-buoy chiffon

Egg yolk batter

1 egg yolk

10 g castor sugar

18 g vegetable/corn oil

22 g water

$^{1}/_{2}$ tsp vanilla extract

26 g cake flour, sifted

Black gel food colouring or $^{3}/_{4}$ tsp charcoal powder

Orange gel food colouring

Meringue

2 egg whites

$^{1}/_{4}$ tsp cream of tartar

22 g castor sugar

Finishing

Marshmallow cream (page 27)

6. Preheat oven to 160°C. Prepare a silicone cake pop mould with 3-cm cavities and a small silicone doughnut mould. Line a 15-cm square baking pan with baking paper.
7. Prepare egg yolk batter (page 20) for boy-in-buoy chiffon. Divide batter into 3 portions, approximately 4 tsp each. To one portion, add black gel food colouring or charcoal powder and mix well for black batter. To another portion, add orange gel food colouring and mix well for orange batter. Leave third portion plain.
8. Prepare meringue (page 20) for boy-in-buoy chiffon. Divide meringue into 3 equal portions, approximately 8 Tbsp each. Gently fold meringue into each batter one-third at a time.
9. Use a small teaspoon to fill half a cake pop cavity with plain batter. Make a wave in batter using the tip of the spoon. Fill remaining space with black batter. Fill another 2 cake pop cavities with plain batter for boy's body and hands. Gently tap mould on counter top to release any air bubbles. Bake at 160°C for 12 minutes. Leave on a wire rack to cool completely before unmoulding.
10. Fill a cavity in doughnut mould with orange batter. Bake at 160°C for 15 minutes or until a skewer inserted into the centre of cake comes out clean. Leave on a wire rack to cool completely before unmoulding.
11. Pour remaining black and plain batters into square baking pan. Gently tap pan on counter top to release any air bubbles. Bake at 160°C for 15 minutes. Invert sheet cake onto a sheet of baking paper and let cool.
12. Peel baking paper from sheet cake and place on a cutting mat. Use bento cutters to cut eyes and mouth from black sheet cake. Arrange on cake pop face using marshmallow cream.
13. Cut 4 strips from plain sheet cake and wrap around doughnut cake to make pattern on life buoy.
14. Use a large straw to cut out two circles from a plain cake pop for hands. Cut boy's body from remaining cake pop by slicing off 2 parallel sides.
15. Assemble boy's body in life buoy, followed by his head and hands using marshmallow cream. Position over hole in cake.

Lemon-Charcoal Busy Bee Cake

Makes one 15-cm cake

Recipe on pages 68 and 69

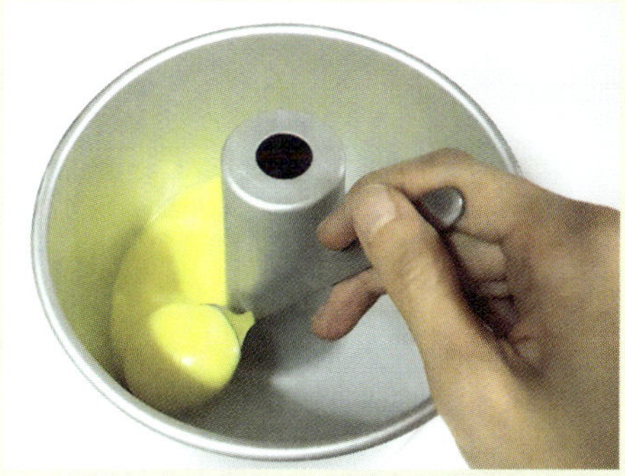

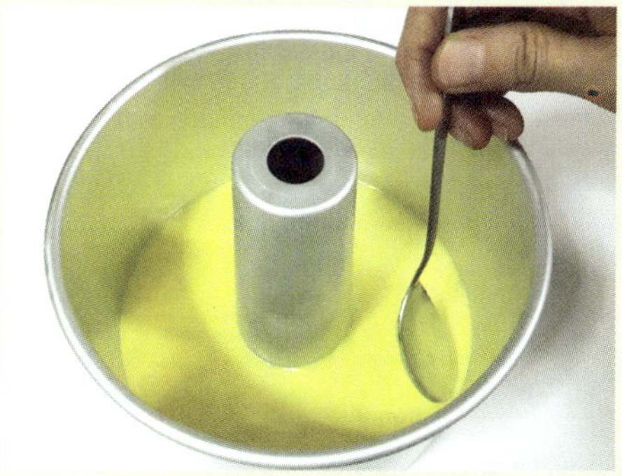

Lemon-charcoal chiffon

Egg yolk batter

4 egg yolks

29 g castor sugar

53 g vegetable/corn oil

31 g lemon juice

31 g water

Zest from 2 lemons

80 g cake flour, sifted

$^1/_3$ tsp lemon emulco

1 tsp charcoal powder or black gel food colouring

Meringue

5 egg whites

$^1/_4$ tsp cream of tartar

60 g castor sugar

1. Preheat oven to 160°C. Prepare a 15-cm chiffon tube pan. Line an 18-cm square baking pan with baking paper.
2. Prepare egg yolk batter (page 20) for lemon-charcoal chiffon. Divide batter into 2 equal portions. Add charcoal powder or black gel food colouring to one portion and mix well. Leave other portion yellow.
3. Prepare meringue (page 20) for lemon-charcoal chiffon. (Ensure that meringue is not overly stiff as batter needs to flow a little.) Divide meringue into 2 equal portions. Gently fold meringue into each batter one-third at a time.
4. Spoon some yellow batter into base of chiffon tube pan until layer is about 1.2 cm thick. Gently level batter. Spoon some black batter over yellow layer gently, taking care not to disturb yellow layer. When layering, begin from the outer ring and work your way towards the inner ring. Repeat to make 5 layers in total ending with a yellow layer. Batter should be about 2 cm from rim of pan. Gently tap pan on counter top to release any air bubbles.
5. Bake at 160°C for 15 minutes, then 140°C for 20–25 minutes, or until a skewer inserted into the centre of cake comes out clean. Invert pan on a wire rack to cool completely before unmoulding.
6. Preheat oven to 160°C. Pour remaining black batter and yellow batter side by side into square baking pan. Gently tap pan on counter top to release any air bubbles.
7. Bake at 160°C for 15 minutes. Invert sheet cake onto a sheet of baking paper and let cool.

Vanilla sheet cake

Egg yolk batter

1 egg yolk

10 g castor sugar

21 g vegetable/corn oil

22 g water

3 g vanilla extract

30 g cake flour, sifted

Pink gel food colouring

Meringue

2 egg whites

$^1/_8$ tsp cream of tartar

23 g castor sugar

Finishing

Marshmallow cream (page 27)

Licorice lace candy

> *Note* Biscuit sticks can be used in place of the licorice lace candy, but do note that the biscuit may soften if the cake is not consumed immediately.

8. Preheat oven to 160°C. Line a 25-cm square baking pan with baking paper.
9. Prepare egg yolk batter (page 20) for vanilla sheet cake. Divide batter into 2 equal portions. Add a little pink gel food colouring to one portion. Leave other portion plain.
10. Prepare meringue (page 20) for vanilla sheet cake. Divide meringue into 2 equal portions. Gently fold meringue into each batter one-third at a time.
11. Pour pink and plain batters side by side into baking pan. Gently tap pan on counter top to release any air bubbles.
12. Bake at 160°C for 15 minutes. Invert sheet cake onto a sheet of baking paper and let cool.
13. Peel baking paper from sheet cakes and place on a cutting mat.
14. Fill centre of tube cake with marshmallows or sweets for a hidden surprise. Cut a circle from yellow sheet cake that is slightly larger than tube hole to ensure a snug fit. Place over tube hole to hide surprise.
15. Use a small round cutter to cut eyes and mouth from black sheet cake. To cut mouth, cut a circle and then make another circular cut 1 mm away.
16. Use a small round cutter to cut rosy cheeks from pink sheet cake. Assemble parts using marshmallow cream.
17. Use a heart-shape cutter to cut 2 hearts from plain sheet cake for wings. Insert a toothpick into the pointed end of each heart cut-out, rotating the toothpick to ease it into cake. Apply marshmallow cream on the pointed end and insert into side of cake.
18. Cut a length of liquorice lace candy into 3-cm strips for feelers. Insert a toothpick into one end of each strip. Cut an 8-mm circle from black sheet cake and stick it to the other end with marshmallow cream. Insert feelers into side of cake.

Cocoa-Pandan Camouflage Cake

Makes one 15-cm round cake
and one 15-cm dome cake

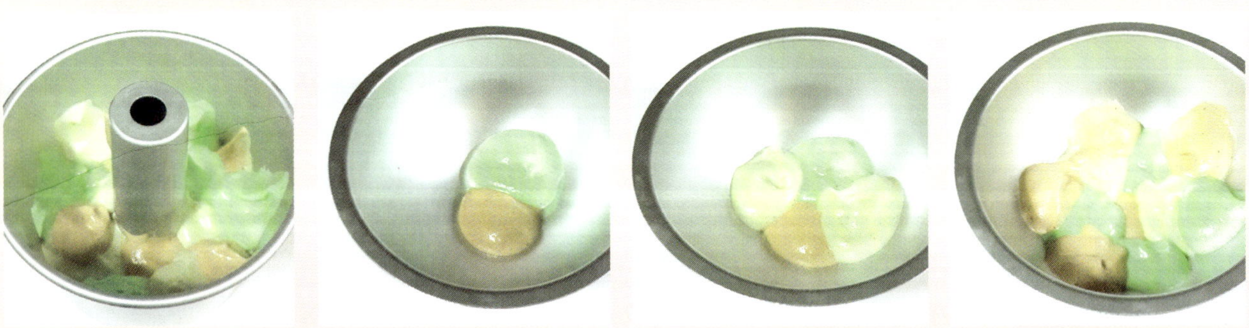

Camouflage chiffon

Egg yolk batter

6 egg yolks

40 g castor sugar

80 g vegetable/corn oil

83 g water

10 g vanilla extract

120 g cake flour, sifted

A pinch of salt

Meringue

8 egg whites

$^1/_4$ tsp cream of tartar

90 g castor sugar

Vanilla sheet cake

Egg yolk batter

$^2/_3$ or 9 g egg yolk

5 g castor sugar

10 g vegetable/corn oil

13 g water

14 g cake flour

Black gel food colouring
or $^1/_2$ tsp charcoal powder

Meringue

1 egg white

A pinch of cream of tartar

10 g castor sugar

Finishing

Marshmallow cream (page 27)

Green	1 tsp pandan paste + 7 g coconut cream powder
Brown	1 tsp cocoa powder + a pinch of baking powder
Dark Green	$^1/_3$ tsp pandan paste + $^1/_3$ tsp cocoa powder

1. Preheat oven to 160°C. Prepare a 15-cm chiffon tube pan and a 15-cm ball cake pan. Line two 15-cm square baking pans with baking paper.
2. Prepare egg yolk batter (page 20). Divide batter into 3 equal portions. Add flavouring for each colour, as suggested in table below, to each bowl. Mix well.
3. Prepare meringue (page 20). Divide meringue into 3 equal portions. Gently fold meringue one-third at a time into each egg yolk batter.
4. Place spoonfuls of each coloured batter randomly into chiffon tube pan and ball cake pan until batter is 2 cm from rim of pans. The blobs should be of different shapes and sizes. Gently tap pans on counter top to release any air bubbles.
5. Bake at 160°C for 15 minutes, then 140°C for 25–26 minutes, or until a skewer inserted into the centre of cakes comes out clean.
6. Invert pans on a wire rack to cool completely before unmoulding.
7. Preheat oven to 160°C. Pour remaining batters onto a square baking pan. Bake at 160°C for 14 minutes. Invert sheet cake onto a sheet of baking paper and let cool.
8. Prepare egg yolk batter for vanilla sheet cake. Add black gel food colouring or charcoal powder. Mix well for black batter.
9. Pour black batter onto baking pan. Gently tap pan on counter top to release any air bubbles. Bake at 160°C for 14 minutes. Invert sheet cake onto a sheet of baking paper and let cool.
10. Fill centre of tube cake with a hidden surprise. Brush marshmallow cream on top surface of cake and place ball cake on tube cake to conceal surprise.
11. Peel baking paper from sheet cakes and place on a cutting mat. Use a large round cutter to cut eyebrows by making 2 cuts 1 mm apart on black sheet cake. Use a small round cutter to cut 2 eyes.
12. Use a daisy cutter to cut flower shapes from green/brown/dark green sheet cakes. Slice flowers in half to create bushes.
13. Assemble parts using marshmallow cream.

Salted Egg Yolk Crab Chiffon with Lava Custard

Makes one 15-cm cake

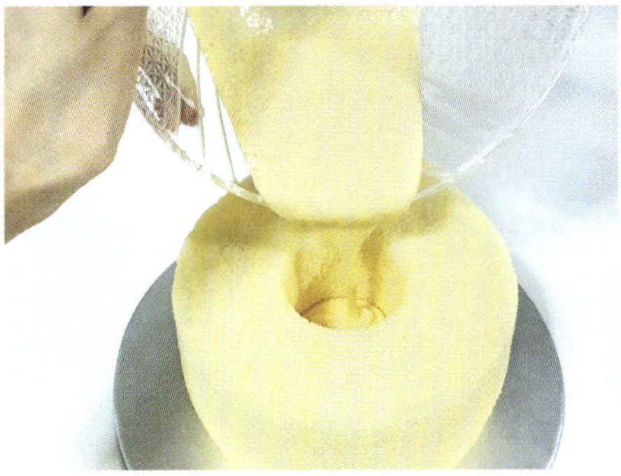

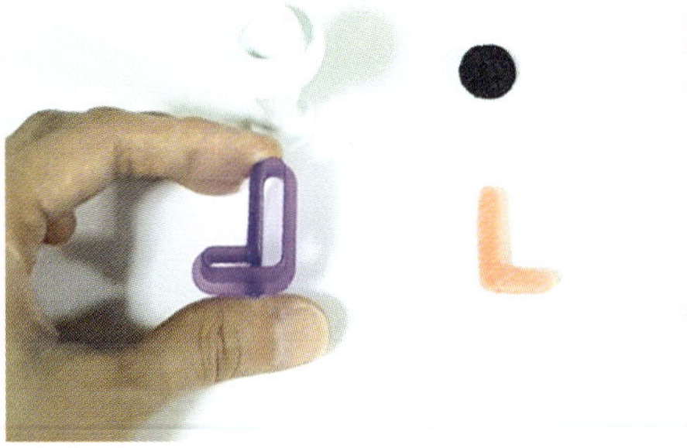

Recipe on pages 74 and 75

Salted egg yolk chiffon

Egg yolk batter

3 salted egg yolks
2 egg yolks
13 g castor sugar
27 g vegetable/corn oil
34 g milk
40 g cake flour
$^{1}/_{6}$ tsp baking powder
$^{1}/_{6}$ tsp salt

Meringue

3 egg whites
30 g castor sugar
$^{1}/_{4}$ tsp cream of tartar

1. Place all 6 salted duck eggs for salted egg yolk chiffon, crab chiffon and salted egg yolk custard in a pot of boiling water and boil until egg yolks turn opaque and are done. Drain well.
2. Place 3 cooked salted egg yolks into a bowl for chiffon cake batter, 2 cooked salted egg yolks in another bowl for crab chiffon and the remaining salted egg yolk into a third bowl for custard. Mash salted egg yolks finely. Set aside.
3. Preheat oven to 160°C. Prepare a 15-cm chiffon tube pan.
4. Prepare egg yolk batter for salted egg yolk chiffon. Whisk egg yolks with sugar until pale in colour. Add oil and milk and mix well. Sift flour, baking powder and salt into mashed salted egg yolks. Mix well and push mixture through a fine mesh sieve. Add to egg yolk batter and mix well.
5. Prepare meringue (page 20). Gently fold meringue into egg yolk batter one-third at a time.
6. Pour batter into tube pan. Gently tap pan on counter top to release any air bubbles.
7. Bake at 160°C for 15 minutes, then 140°C for 25–30 minutes, or until a skewer inserted into the centre of cake comes out clean.
8. Invert pan on a wire rack to cool completely before unmoulding.

Crab chiffon

Egg yolk batter

2 salted egg yolks

2 egg yolks

13 g castor sugar

27 g vegetable/corn oil

34 g milk

40 g cake flour

1/6 tsp baking powder

1/6 tsp salt

1/3 tsp red yeast powder or a little red gel food colouring

1/4 tsp charcoal powder

Meringue

3 egg whites

30 g castor sugar

1/4 tsp cream of tartar

Salted egg yolk custard

1 salted egg yolk

25 g unsalted butter, melted and lightly cooled

25 g icing sugar

7 g custard powder

1/2 tsp salt

55 g milk

Finishing

Marshmallow cream (page 27)

9. Prepare an 8-cm round glass bowl, a silicone cake pop mould with 3-cm cavities. Line a 15-cm square baking pan with baking paper. Preheat oven to 160°C.
10. Prepare egg yolk batter (page 20) for crab chiffon. Spoon 2 tsp batter each into 2 bowls. Add charcoal powder to one bowl and mix well for black batter. Leave other portion plain. Add red yeast powder or red food gel food colouring to remaining batter and mix well for red batter.
11. Prepare meringue (page 20) for crab chiffon. Gently fold meringue one-third at a time into respective egg yolk batters: 4 Tbsp each into black and plain batters and remaining meringue into red batter.
12. Pour red batter into prepared glass bowl until batter is about 1.5 cm from rim of bowl. Gently tap bowl on counter top to release any air bubbles. Bake at 160°C for 15 minutes, then 150°C for 15 minutes, or until a skewer inserted into the centre of cake comes out clean. Invert bowl on a wire rack to cool completely before unmoulding.
13. Spoon plain batter equally into 2 cavities in cake pop mould for eyes. Repeat with red batter for pincers. Bake at 160°C for 12 minutes. Leave to cool on a wire rack before unmoulding.
14. Pour remaining red batter and black batter side by side into prepared baking pan. Bake at 160°C for 14 minutes. Invert sheet cake onto a sheet of baking paper and let cool.
15. Prepare salted egg yolk custard. Using an electric mixer, beat butter and icing sugar at medium speed until well-mixed. Lower mixing speed, add remaining ingredients and mix until well-combined.
16. Fill centre of cake with salted egg yolk custard. Place bowl cake over as body of crab to conceal custard.
17. Peel baking paper from sheet cake and place on a cutting mat. Use a round cutter to cut out 2 circles from black sheet cake for eye balls. Use a L letter cutter to cut out 8 legs from red sheet cake.
18. Cut a wedge from red cake pops to create shape of pincers.
19. Insert toothpicks into pincers and eyes, then insert into position in bowl cake. Assemble eye balls on eyes and stick 4 legs on each side of crab using marshmallow cream.

Orange Chick Chiffon

Makes one 18-cm cake

Recipe on pages 78 and 79

Orange chiffon

Egg yolk batter

3 egg yolks

20 g castor sugar

39 g vegetable/corn oil

48 g orange juice or mandarin orange juice

Zest from $1^{1}/_{2}$ oranges or mandarin oranges

A few drops of orange emulco

60 g cake flour, sifted

A pinch of baking powder

A pinch of salt

$^{1}/_{3}$ tsp charcoal powder mixed with $^{1}/_{3}$ tsp cake flour

Meringue

4 egg whites

$^{1}/_{4}$ tsp cream of tartar

45 g castor sugar

1. Preheat oven to 160°C. Prepare an 18-cm chiffon tube pan.
2. Prepare egg yolk batter (page 20) for orange chiffon. Spoon 1 tsp batter into a small bowl. Add charcoal powder and cake flour mixture and mix well for black batter.
3. Prepare meringue (page 20) for orange chiffon. Gently fold meringue into each batter one-third at a time: 2 Tbsp meringue into black batter and remainder into orange batter.
4. Spoon black batter into a piping bag and cut a 2-cm hole at the tip. Pipe 2 dots on the base of chiffon tube pan for chick's eyes. Bake at 160°C for $1^{1}/_{2}$ minutes.
5. Pour orange batter into chiffon tube pan until batter is 2 cm from rim of pan. Gently tap pan on counter top to release any air bubbles.
6. Bake at 160°C for 15 minutes, then 140°C for 30 minutes, or until a skewer inserted into the centre of cake comes out clean.
7. Invert pan on a wire rack to cool completely before unmoulding.
8. Preheat oven to 160°C. Line a 25-cm square baking pan with baking paper.

Coloured sheet cake

Egg yolk batter

1 egg yolk

10 g castor sugar

21 g vegetable/corn oil

27 g orange juice
(or mandarin orange juice)

30 g cake flour, sifted

Red gel food colouring

Orange emulco

Meringue

2 egg whites

1/8 tsp cream of tartar

23 g castor sugar

Finishing

Marshmallow cream (page 27)

9. Prepare egg yolk batter (page 20) for coloured sheet cake. Spoon 3 tsp batter into a small bowl and add a drop of red gel food colouring for red batter. Spoon 5 tsp batter into a second bowl and add few drops of orange emulco for light orange batter. Add 1/4 tsp orange emulco to remaining batter for a deep orange batter.
10. Prepare meringue (page 20) for coloured sheet cake. Gently fold meringue into each batter one-third at a time: 6 Tbsp meringue into red batter, 10 Tbsp meringue into light orange batter and remaining meringue into deep orange batter.
11. Pour coloured batters side by side onto baking pan. Gently tap pan on counter top to release any air bubbles.
12. Bake at 160°C for 15 minutes. Invert sheet cake onto a sheet of baking paper and let cool.
13. Peel baking paper from sheet cake and place on a cutting mat.
14. Use a flower cutter to cut 2 flower shapes from light orange sheet cake, then slice off sides leaving a fan shape for chick's wings. Insert a toothpick into cut-outs. Brush pointed end of wings with marshmallow cream and insert into side of cake. Repeat this step with deep orange sheet cake for chick's feet. Repeat again but making only one cut-out with red sheet cake for comb on chick's head.
15. Use a large square cutter to cut a square from the deep orange sheet cake, then slice in half for chick's beak.
16. Assemble parts on cake using marshmallow cream. Use a pink food marker to add rosy cheeks.

AND MADE
Best Quality

Sugar & Spice & Everything Nice

Six-Flavour Earth Tones Blossom Cake

Makes one 18-cm cake

Recipe on pages 84 and 85

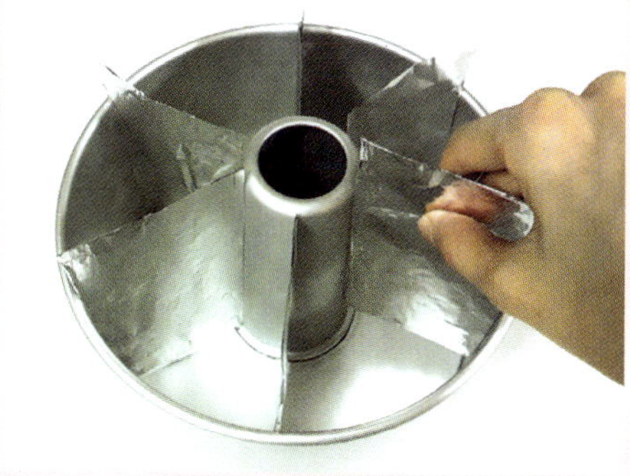

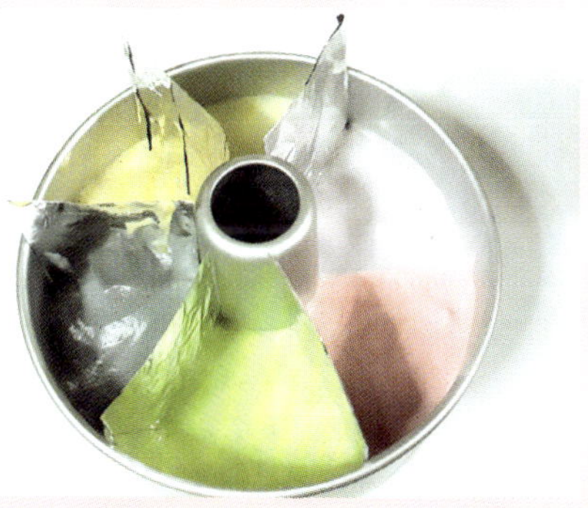

Six-flavour cake

Egg yolk batter

4 egg yolks

27 g castor sugar

47 g vegetable/corn oil

53 g water

80 g cake flour, sifted

A pinch of baking powder

Meringue

6 egg whites

$^1/_4$ tsp cream of tartar

60 g castor sugar

1. Prepare an 18-cm round chiffon tube pan. Foil 6 sheets of aluminium foil into rectangular sheets corresponding to the radius of chiffon pan.
2. Preheat oven to 160°C.
3. Prepare egg yolk batter (page 20) for 6-flavour cake. Spoon batter equally into 6 small bowls. Add flavouring and colours to each bowl as suggested in table below. Mix well to get 6 different batters.
4. Prepare meringue (page 20). Divide meringue into 6 equal portions and gently fold into each egg yolk batter one-third at a time.
5. Arrange aluminium foil dividers vertically in chiffon pan to create 6 equal segments.
6. Spoon a different batter into each segment, doing this gently but quickly to avoid deflating batter.
7. Remove aluminium foil dividers gently with both hands, being careful to keep the foil vertical to ensure the resulting line between the batters is straight.
8. Bake at 160°C for 15 minutes, then 140°C for 30 minutes, or until a skewer inserted into the centre of cake comes out clean.

Suggested Asian Flavours and Earth Tones	
Matcha	$1^1/_5$ tsp matcha dissolved in 6 g hot milk
Adzuki	11 g smooth adzuki bean paste + a drop of red or pink colouring + a pinch of baking powder
Coffee/ Cocoa	$1^1/_2$ tsp instant coffee powder or $1^1/_2$ tsp cocoa powder dissolved in 6 g hot milk
Charcoal	$^1/_4$ tsp charcoal powder dissolved in 6 g hot milk
Soy	2 tsp soy milk powder dissolved in 6 g hot soy milk
Yam	2 tsp yam powder dissolved in 6 g hot milk

Suggested Flavouring and Rainbow Colours	
Red	1 tsp strawberry purée + $^1/_5$ tsp strawberry paste
Orange	1 tsp orange juice + zest from $^1/_3$ orange + $^1/_5$ tsp orange paste
Yellow	1 tsp lemon juice + zest from $^1/_3$ lemon + $^1/_5$ tsp lemon paste
Green	1 tsp pandan juice + $^1/_5$ tsp pandan paste
Blue	1 tsp blue pea flower extract + $^1/_5$ tsp vanilla extract + a little blue gel food colouring
Purple	$^1/_2$ tsp blueberry powder + $^2/_5$ blueberry extract + $^4/_5$ tsp water

Flower sheet cake

Egg yolk batter

1 egg yolk

7 g castor sugar

13 g vegetable/corn oil

19 g water

20 g cake flour, sifted

A little pink gel food colouring

Meringue

$1^{1}/_{2}$ egg whites (60 g)

$^{1}/_{4}$ tsp cream of tartar

15 g castor sugar

Finishing

Marshmallow cream (page 27)

9. Invert pan on a wire rack to cool completely before unmoulding.
10. Preheat oven to 160°C. Line a 23-cm baking pan with baking paper.
11. Prepare egg yolk batter (page 20) and meringue (page 20) for flower sheet cake. Gently fold meringue into egg yolk batter one-third at a time.
12. Pour batter onto prepared pan. Gently tap pan on counter top to release any air bubbles.
13. Bake at 160°C for 15 minutes. Invert sheet cake onto a sheet of baking paper and let cool.
14. Peel baking paper from sheet cake and place on a cutting mat. Use a flower cutter to cut out flower shapes.
15. Adhere flowers onto cake using marshmallow cream.

Yuzu Rainbow Hearts Chiffon Pops

Makes 6 cake pops

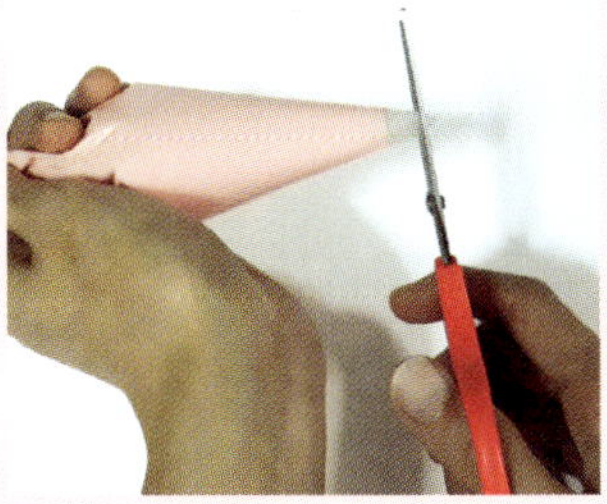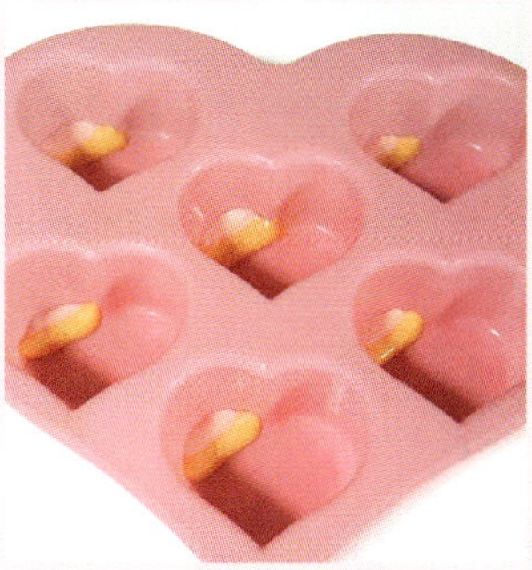

Egg yolk batter

2¼ Tbsp yuzu jam/ honey citron tea
36 g hot water

2 egg yolks

11 g castor sugar

27 g vegetable/corn oil

40 g cake flour, sifted

A pinch of salt

Pink, orange, yellow, green, blue and purple gel food colouring

Meringue

3 egg whites

¼ tsp cream of tartar

30 g castor sugar

> *Note* When inserting the cake pop stick into the cake, it helps to twist the stick as you push it in. This will also ensure that the cake maintains its shape.

1. Make yuzu tea by dissolving yuzu jam/honey citron tea in 36 g hot water, then straining to remove yuzu bits. (This is because the yuzu bits may distort the layers). Measure out 32 g yuzu tea for use in egg yolk batter. Leave to cool before using.
2. Preheat oven to 160°C. Prepare a silicone heart mould with 6-cm wide cavities.
3. Prepare egg yolk batter. Divide batter into 6 equal portions and add a different gel food colouring to each portion. Mix well.
4. Prepare meringue. Divide meringue into 6 equal portions and gently fold into each egg yolk batter one-third at a time.
5. Spoon each batter into a separate piping bag and cut a 2-mm hole at the tip of each bag.
6. Pipe a diagonal line across the base of each cavity using pink batter. Pipe a second line beside the first using orange batter, and continue with yellow, green, blue and purple batters or in an order of your preference. When the first layer is complete, repeat to pipe another 3–4 layers in the same order until the batter is about 2 cm thick.
7. Bake at 160°C for 10 minutes, then 140°C for 10–15 minutes, or until a skewer inserted into the centre of cakes comes out clean.
8. Leave on a wire rack to cool completely before unmoulding and inserting cake pops sticks.

Lavender Hydrangea Cupcakes

Makes 4 cupcakes

Note To make bouquets, bake the batter for the mound cupcakes in four cones and four 5-cm cake pop cavities.

Mound cupcakes

Egg yolk batter

1 tsp dried lavender flowers

47 g boiling water/milk

3 egg yolks

20 g castor sugar

39 g vegetable/corn oil

60 g cake flour, sifted

Meringue

4 egg whites

$^{1}/_{4}$ tsp cream of tartar

45 g castor sugar

Flowers & leaves sheet cakes

Egg yolk batter

$1^{1}/_{3}$ tsp dried lavender flowers

63 g boiling water/milk

4 egg yolks

27 g castor sugar

52 g vegetable/corn oil

80 g cake flour, sifted

Purple and green gel food colouring

Meringue

5 egg whites

$^{1}/_{4}$ tsp cream of tartar

60 g castor sugar

Finishing

Marshmallow cream (page 27)

Candy beads

1. Prepare lavender extract for both cupcake and sheet cake. Steep lavender flowers in boiling water/milk for at least 5 minutes.
2. Preheat oven to 160°C. Prepare four 11-cm glass bowls.
3. Prepare egg yolk batter (page 20) and meringue (page 20) for mound cupcakes. Gently fold meringue into egg yolk batter one-third at a time.
4. Pour batter equally into glass bowls until batter is 1.5 cm from rim of bowls. Gently tap bowls on counter top to release any air bubbles. Bake at 160°C for 15 minutes, then 150°C for 15 minutes or until a skewer inserted into the centre of cakes comes out clean. Invert moulds on a wire rack to cool completely before unmoulding.
5. Preheat oven to 160°C. Line two 25-cm square baking pans and one 20-cm square baking pan with baking paper.
6. Prepare egg yolk batter (page 20) for sheet cakes. Spoon 10 tsp batter into another bowl and add a little green gel food colouring. Mix well. Divide remaining batter equally between 2 bowls. Add a little purple gel food colouring to one portion and a little more purple gel food colouring to the other for a darker shade. Mix well.
7. Prepare meringue (page 20) for sheet cakes. Gently fold meringue into respective egg yolk batters one-third at a time: 20 Tbsp meringue into green batter, and remaining meringue divided equally between purple batters (about 30 Tbsp each).
8. Pour purple batters into 25-cm baking pans and green batter into 20-cm baking pan. Gently tap pans on counter top to release any air bubbles. Bake at 160°C for 15 minutes. Invert sheet cakes onto baking paper and let cool.
9. Peel baking paper from sheet cakes and place on a cutting mat. Use a leaf cutter to cut leaves from green sheet cake. Use a flower cutter to cut flowers from purple sheet cakes. Assemble leaves and flowers on mound cake using marshmallow cream. Finish with candy beads for flower centres.

Neapolitan Chiffon Doughnuts

Makes 8 doughnuts

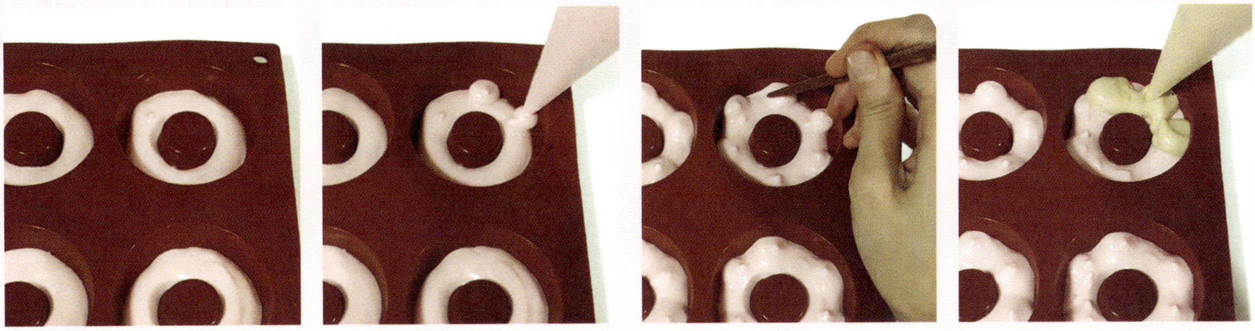

Egg yolk batter

2 egg yolks
13 g castor sugar
25 g vegetable/corn oil
28 g milk
3 g vanilla extract
40 g cake flour, sifted
1/4 tsp chocolate emulco
1/4 tsp strawberry paste

Meringue

3 egg whites
1/4 tsp cream of tartar
30 g castor sugar

Finishing

Sugar sprinkles or dragée
Marshmallow cream (page 27)

1. Preheat oven to 160°C. Prepare a silicone doughnut mould with 6-cm cavities.
2. Prepare egg yolk batter (page 20). Divide batter into 2 equal portions. Add chocolate emulco to one portion and strawberry paste to the other. Mix well.
3. Prepare meringue (page 20). Divide meringue into 2 equal portions and gently fold into each egg yolk batter one-third at a time.
4. Spoon batters into separate piping bags and cut a 2-mm hole at the tip of each bag.
5. Pipe strawberry batter to fill a third of each cavity in doughnut mould. Pipe 6 small mounds at the outer edge of each doughnut, then smoothen sides using a chopstick to create frosting on doughnuts.
6. Pipe chocolate batter over strawberry batter until cavities are full. Gently tap mould on counter top to release any air bubbles.
7. Bake at 160°C for 10 minutes, then 140°C for 5–10 minutes, or until a skewer inserted into the centre of cakes comes out clean. Leave on a wire rack to cool completely before unmoulding.
8. Decorate with sugar sprinkles or dragée and adhere using marshmallow cream.

Milk & Chocolate Neko Chiffon Doughnuts

Makes 6 doughnuts

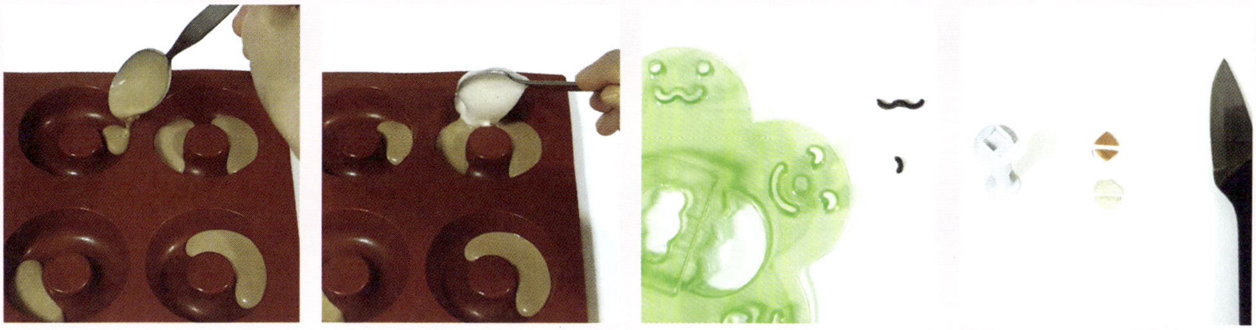

Egg yolk batter

1 egg

20 g castor sugar

40 g vegetable/corn oil

45 g hot milk

60 g cake flour, sifted

1/2 tsp charcoal powder or black gel food colouring

18 g chocolate malt powder + a pinch of baking powder, mixed with 15 g hot milk to form a smooth paste

Meringue

4 egg whites

1/4 tsp cream of tartar

45 g castor sugar

Finishing

Marshmallow cream (page 27)

> *Note* This is a special reduced egg yolk recipe to produce a lighter coloured cake.

1. Preheat oven to 160°C. Prepare a silicone doughnut mould with 6-cm cavities. Line a 23-cm square baking pan with baking paper.
2. Prepare egg yolk batter (page 20). Spoon 7 tsp batter into a small bowl and add charcoal powder or black gel food colouring. Mix well for a black batter. Spoon 12 tsp batter into another bowl and add chocolate malt paste. Mix well for a brown batter. Leave remaining batter plain.
3. Prepare meringue (page 20). Gently fold meringue into each batter one-third at a time: 14 Tbsp meringue into black batter, 24 Tbsp meringue into brown batter and remaining meringue into plain batter.
4. Use a small teaspoon to spoon brown batter randomly into 6 cavities in doughnut mould, then top with plain batter until cavities are full.
5. Bake at 160°C for 10 minutes, then 140°C for 5–10 minutes, or until a skewer inserted into the centre of cakes comes out clean. Leave to cool on a wire rack before unmoulding.
6. Pour leftover brown, plain and black batters side by side into baking pan. Gently tap pan on counter top to release any air bubbles. Bake at 160°C for 15 minutes. Invert sheet cake onto a sheet of baking paper and let cool.
7. Peel baking paper from sheet cake and place on a cutting mat. Use bento cutters to cut cats' facial features from black sheet cake. Use a small square cutter to cut squares from brown and plain sheet cakes, then cut into triangles for cats' ears. Adhere to doughnuts using marshmallow cream.

Passion Fruit Lollipop Chiffon Pops

Makes 12 cake pops

Egg yolk batter

2 egg yolks

10 g castor sugar

25 g vegetable/corn oil

32 g passion fruit juice

40 g cake flour, sifted + 1/4 tsp extra for mixing into plain batter

Pink, blue, green, yellow gel or natural food colouring

Meringue

3 egg whites

1/4 tsp cream of tartar

30 g castor sugar

> *Note* For a different flavour, replace the passion fruit juice with any fruit juice of your choice such as yuzu juice.

1. Preheat oven to 160°C. Prepare 12 waxed cupcake cases, each 3.5-cm wide.
2. Prepare egg yolk batter (page 20). Spoon 2 tsp batter into a small bowl. Add 1/4 tsp cake flour and mix well for plain batter. Spoon remaining batter equally into another 4 small bowls (about 4 1/2 tsp each) and mix a different food colouring into each portion.
3. Prepare meringue (page 20). Gently fold meringue into each batter one-third at a time: 5 Tbsp meringue into plain batter and remaining meringue equally into each coloured batter (about 9 Tbsp each).
4. Spoon batters into separate piping bags and cut a 2-mm hole at the tip of each bag.
5. Use plain batter to pipe a swirl into the base of a cupcake case. Fill spaces between plain swirl with pink batter, starting from the inside and following the plain swirl outwards. Then, fill cupcake case with pink batter until batter is about 1.2 cm thick. Repeat to make 3 lollipops of each colour.
6. Bake at 160°C for 12–15 minutes, or until a skewer inserted into the centre of cakes comes out clean.
7. Leave cakes to cool completely on a wire rack before unmoulding and inserting cake pop sticks.

Ice Cream Chiffon Pops with Vanilla Centres

Makes 5 cake pops

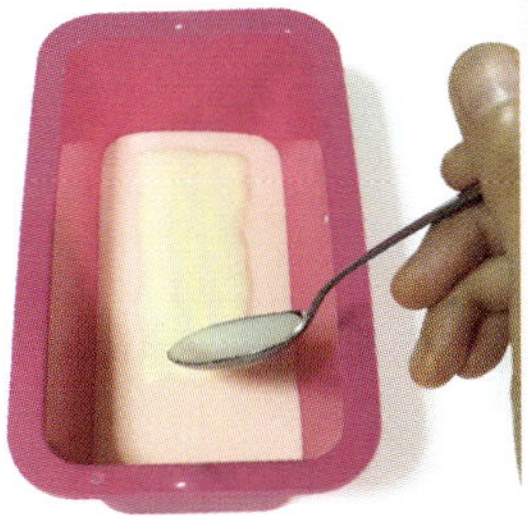

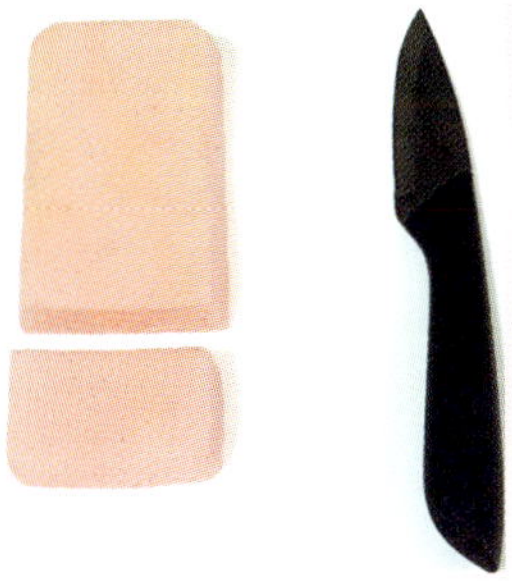

Egg yolk batter

3 egg yolks

20 g castor sugar

39 g vegetable/corn oil

47 g water

60 g cake flour, sifted

Flavours

1 g vanilla extract

1 g strawberry paste

1 g pandan paste

1 g lemon paste

1 g blue pea flower extract (page 28) + a little blue gel food colouring

Meringue

4 egg whites

1/4 tsp cream of tartar

45 g castor sugar

> *Note* The plain batter for the vanilla centre does not need to be spread down the full length of the pan as the cake will be trimmed to shorten it after baking.

1. Preheat oven to 160°C. Prepare four 5-cm x 11-cm rectangular silicone baking pans.
2. Prepare egg yolk batter (page 20). Spoon 3 tsp batter into a small bowl for plain batter. Divide remaining batter equally among another 4 small bowls (about 7 tsp batter each). Mix vanilla extract into plain batter and a different flavour/colouring into each of the other portions.
3. Prepare meringue (page 20). Gently fold meringue into each batter one-third at a time: 6 Tbsp meringue into plain batter and remaining meringue equally into each flavoured/coloured batter (about 14 Tbsp each).
4. Spoon strawberry batter into a baking pan until batter is about 5 mm thick. Gently spoon some plain batter over strawberry batter, leaving a margin all around, with a thicker margin at one short end, to create vanilla centre in ice cream pop. Spoon a thin layer of strawberry batter over to complete ice cream pop. Repeat step using remaining batter.
5. Bake at 160°C for 10 minutes, then 140°C for 5–10 minutes, or until a skewer inserted into the centre of cakes comes out clean. Leave cakes to cool completely on a wire rack before unmoulding.
6. Place cakes on a cutting mat. Trim a quarter off one end of cakes where the vanilla centre stops. This is optional, as I prefer to have the cakes shorter. Use a fluted (oval or round) cutter to trim a corner of cake to reveal vanilla centre.
7. Insert cake pop sticks.

Chocolate Hazelnut-Strawberry Giant Cupcake

Makes one 15-cm round cake
and one 15-cm dome cake

Recipe on pages 100 and 101

Chocolate hazelnut chiffon

Egg yolk batter

60 g milk

105 g chocolate hazelnut spread

3 egg yolks

$^{1}/_{3}$ tsp vanilla extract

48 g cake flour, sifted

A pinch of baking powder

Meringue

3 egg whites

48 g castor sugar

$^{1}/_{4}$ tsp cream of tartar

1. In a saucepan, heat milk and add chocolate hazelnut spread. Stir over low heat until spread has completely dissolved and mixture is smooth. Set aside to cool before using in egg yolk batter.
2. Preheat oven to 160°C. Prepare a 15-cm chiffon tube pan.
3. Prepare egg yolk batter (page 20) and meringue (page 20) for chocolate hazelnut chiffon. Gently fold meringue into egg yolk batter one-third at a time.
4. Pour batter into chiffon pan until batter is about 2 cm from rim of pan. Gently tap pan on counter top to release any air bubbles.
5. Bake at 160°C for 15 minutes, then 140°C for 30–35 minutes, or until a skewer inserted into the centre of cake comes out clean.
6. Invert pan on a wire rack to cool completely before unmoulding.

Strawberry-vanilla chiffon

Egg yolk batter

1 egg yolk

17 g castor sugar

37 g vegetable/corn oil

40 g water

5 g vanilla extract

53 g cake flour, sifted

$^1/_4$ tsp + $^1/_4$ tsp strawberry paste

Blue gel food colouring

Meringue

4 egg whites

$^1/_4$ tsp cream of tartar

45 g castor sugar

Finishing

Marshmallow cream (page 27)

7. Preheat oven to 160°C. Prepare a 15-cm ball cake pan and a silicone cake pop mould with 3-cm cavities. Line a 15-cm baking pan with baking paper.
8. Prepare egg yolk batter (page 20) for strawberry-vanilla chiffon. Spoon 1 tsp batter into a small bowl and add $^1/_4$ tsp strawberry paste. Mix well for red batter. Spoon 8 tsp batter into another bowl and add a little blue gel food colouring. Mix well for a light blue batter. Divide remaining batter equally between 2 bowls (about 5 Tbsp each). To one portion, add $^1/_4$ tsp strawberry paste and mix well for pink batter.
9. Prepare meringue (page 20) for strawberry-vanilla chiffon. Gently fold meringue into each batter one-third at a time: 2 Tbsp for red batter, 16 Tbsp for light blue batter and remaining meringue equally into pink and plain batters.
10. Pour some plain batter into ball cake pan to create a base layer about 2 cm thick. With remaining plain batter, create mounds by dropping spoonfuls of batter at intervals, close to sides of pan. Smoothen edge of mounds using a chopstick.
11. Spoon pink batter to fill spaces between mounds until batter is about 2 cm from rim of pan.
12. Bake at 160°C for 15 minutes, then 140°C for 20–25 minutes, or until a skewer inserted into the centre of cake comes out clean. Invert pan on a wire rack to cool completely before unmoulding.
13. Spoon red batter into a cavity in cake pop mould. Bake at 160°C for 12 minutes.
14. Spoon light blue batter into baking pan. Gently tap pan on counter top to release any air bubbles. Bake at 160°C for 15 minutes. Invert sheet cake onto a sheet of baking paper and let cool.
15. Make vertical cuts along sides of chocolate hazelnut chiffon with a sharp knife to create lines of cupcake case. Fill centre of tube cake with marshmallows or sweets for a hidden surprise. Brush top surface of cake with marshmallow cream and place strawberry-vanilla bowl cake over as top of cupcake.
16. Peel baking paper from sheet cake and place on a cutting mat. Use an 'I' letter cutter to cut out sprinkles. Decorate cupcake with sprinkles using marshmallow cream.
17. Place red cake pop on bowl cake for a cherry and adhere using marshmallow cream.

Neapolitan Mushroom Cake

Makes one 15-cm round cake and one 21-cm dome cake

Recipe on pages 104 and 105

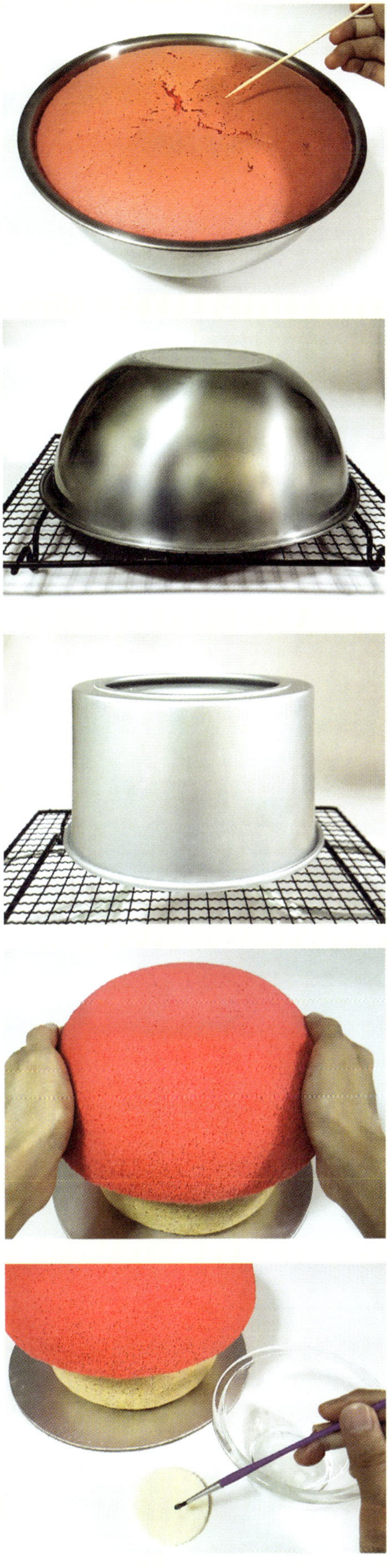

Strawberry chiffon

Egg yolk batter

4 egg yolks

27 g castor sugar

53 g vegetable/corn oil

60 g strawberry puree

72 g cake flour, sifted

8 g red yeast powder

1 tsp strawberry paste

Meringue

5 egg whites

1/4 tsp cream of tartar

56 g castor sugar

1. Preheat oven to 160°C. Prepare a 21-cm heatproof metal bowl.
2. Prepare egg yolk batter (page 20) and meringue (page 20) for strawberry chiffon. Gently fold meringue into egg yolk batter one-third at a time.
3. Pour batter into bowl until batter is 2.5 cm from rim of bowl. Gently tap bowl on counter top to release any air bubbles.
4. Bake cake at 160°C for 15 minutes, 150°C for 30 minutes, then 140°C for 25 minutes, or until a skewer inserted into the centre of cake comes out clean.
5. Invert pan on a wire rack to cool completely before unmoulding.

Chocolate chiffon

Egg yolk batter

2 egg yolks
17 g castor sugar
30 g vegetable/corn oil
33 g water
1 tsp vanilla extract
40 g cake flour, sifted
13 g cocoa powder, sifted
1/4 tsp baking powder
A pinch of salt

Meringue

3 egg whites
1/4 tsp cream of tartar
30 g castor sugar

Vanilla sheet cake

Egg yolk batter

1 egg yolk
7 g castor sugar
13 g vegetable/corn oil
14 g water
1/2 tsp vanilla extract
20 g cake flour, sifted

Meringue

1 1/2 egg whites (60 g)
1/4 tsp cream of tartar
15 g castor sugar

Finishing

Marshmallow cream (page 27)

6. Preheat oven to 160°C. Prepare a 15-cm chiffon tube pan.
7. Prepare egg yolk batter (page 20) and meringue (page 20) for chocolate chiffon. Gently fold meringue into egg yolk batter one-third at a time.
8. Pour batter into pan until batter is 2 cm from rim of pan. Gently tap pan on counter top to release any air bubbles.
9. Bake at 160°C for 15 minutes, then 140°C for 25 minutes, or until a skewer inserted into the centre of cake comes out clean.
10. Invert pan to cool completely on a wire rack before unmoulding.
11. Preheat oven to 160°C. Line a 20-cm square baking pan with baking paper.
12. Prepare egg yolk batter (page 20) and meringue (page 20) for vanilla sheet cake. Gently fold meringue into egg yolk batter one-third at a time.
13. Pour vanilla batter into baking pan. Bake at 160°C for 15 minutes. Invert sheet cake onto a sheet of baking paper and let cool.
14. Fill centre of tube cake with marshmallows or sweets for a hidden surprise. Brush top surface of cake with marshmallow cream and place red bowl cake over as cap of mushroom.
15. Peel baking paper from vanilla sheet cake and place on a cutting mat. Use round cutters to cut circles from sheet cake for spots on mushroom. Adhere to red bowl cake using marshmallow cream.

happy

Come On & Celebrate!

Soy-Pandan Christmas Wreath Cake

Makes one 23-cm Bundt cake

Note I've used soy milk in this recipe for its lovely flavour. It is also a healthier alternative to coconut milk, but it can be replaced with coconut milk if preferred.

Suggested Flavouring and Colours	
Dark Green	$^{1}/_{3}$ tsp pandan paste + $^{1}/_{5}$ tsp charcoal powder
Red	$^{1}/_{2}$ tsp red yeast powder or red gel food colouring

Soy-pandan chiffon

Egg yolk batter

4 egg yolks
27 g castor sugar
52 g vegetable/corn/coconut oil
52 g soy milk
4 g vanilla extract
2 tsp pandan paste
80 g cake flour
A pinch of salt
2 tsp soy powder (optional)

Meringue

5 egg whites
1/4 tsp cream of tartar
60 g sugar

Pandan sheet cakes

Egg yolk batter

3 egg yolks
20 g castor sugar
39 g vegetable/corn/coconut oil
39 g soy milk
1/2 tsp vanilla extract
1 tsp pandan paste
60 g cake flour
A pinch of salt

Meringue

4 egg whites
1/4 tsp cream of tartar
45 g castor sugar

Finishing

Marshmallow cream (page 27)

1. Preheat oven to 160°C. Prepare a 23-cm silicone Bundt pan.
2. Prepare egg yolk batter (page 20) and meringue (page 20) for soy-pandan chiffon. Gently fold meringue into egg yolk batter one-third at a time.
3. Pour soy-pandan batter into Bundt pan until batter is about 4 cm from rim of pan. Gently tap pan on counter top to release any air bubbles.
4. Bake at 160°C for 15 minutes, 150°C for 5 minutes, then 140°C, for 25–30 minutes, or until a skewer inserted into the centre of cake comes out clean. Invert pan on a wire rack to cool completely before unmoulding.
5. Prepare pandan sheet cakes. Preheat oven to 160°C. Line three 20-cm square baking pans with baking paper.
6. Prepare egg yolk batter (page 20) for sheet cakes. Divide batter into three equal portions. Add colouring as suggested in table to 2 bowls and mix well. Leave third portion light green.
7. Prepare meringue (page 20) for sheet cakes. Divide meringue into three equal portions. Gently fold meringue one-third at a time into each egg yolk batter.
8. Pour each batter into a separate baking pan. Gently tap pan on counter top to release any air bubbles. Bake at 160°C for 15 minutes. Invert each sheet cake onto a sheet of baking paper and let cool.
9. Peel baking paper from sheet cakes and place on a cutting mat. Use a holly leaf cutter to cut leaves from light and dark green sheet cakes. Use a flower cutter, circle cutter and bow cutter to cut flowers, berries and a bow from red sheet cake.
10. Arrange leaves, flowers, berries and bow on Bundt cake and adhere using marshmallow cream.

Dark Chocolate & Mint Christmas Pull-Apart Cupcakes

Makes 17 cupcakes

Recipe on pages 112 and 113

Dark chocolate chiffon cupcakes

Egg yolk batter

78 g dark chocolate, chopped
3 egg yolks
36 g vegetable/corn oil
68 g milk
34 g cake flour, sifted
15 g cocoa powder, sifted
1/4 tsp baking powder
1/4 tsp baking soda

Meringue

4 egg whites
1/4 tsp cream of tartar
52 g castor sugar

Mint sheet cakes

Egg yolk batter

4 egg yolks
46 g castor sugar
52 g vegetable/corn oil
55 g water
1/4 tsp vanilla extract
80 g cake flour
1/3 tsp cocoa powder, sifted
1 tsp peppermint extract
Green gel food colouring

Meringue

5 egg whites
1/4 tsp cream of tartar
60 g castor sugar

1. Preheat oven to 160°C. Prepare 17 waxed cupcake cases.
2. Melt dark chocolate in a double boiler and stir until smooth. Set aside to cool a little.
3. Prepare egg yolk batter (page 20) and meringue (page 20) for dark chocolate chiffon. Gently fold meringue into egg yolk batter one-third at a time. Fill cupcake cases until batter is about 1 cm from rim of cases.
4. Bake at 160°C for 10 minutes, then 150°C for 7–10 minutes, or until a skewer inserted into the centre of cakes comes out clean. Let cool.
5. Prepare mint sheet cakes. Preheat oven to 160°C. Line two 25-cm square baking pans and one 15-cm square baking pan with baking paper.
6. Prepare egg yolk batter (page 20) for mint sheet cakes. Spoon 8 tsp batter into a small bowl and add cocoa powder. To remaining batter, add peppermint extract and a little green gel food colouring.
7. Prepare meringue (page 20) for mint sheet cakes. Gently fold meringue one-third at a time into respective egg yolk batters: 16 Tbsp meringue into dark chocolate batter and remaining meringue into mint batter.
8. Pour mint batter equally into two 25-cm baking pans. Pour dark chocolate batter into 15-cm baking pan. Gently tap pans on counter top to release any air bubbles. Bake at 160°C for 15 minutes. Invert each sheet cake onto a sheet of baking paper and let cool.

Colourful chiffon pops

Egg yolk batter

2 egg yolks

13 g castor sugar

26 g vegetable/corn oil

28 g water

3/4 tsp vanilla extract

40 g cake flour, sifted

Pink, yellow, blue and purple gel food colouring

Meringue

3 egg whites

1/4 tsp cream of tartar

30 g castor sugar

Finishing

Marshmallow cream (page 27)

String candy

9. Prepare a silicone cake pop mould with 3-cm cavities. Line a 15-cm square baking pan with baking paper.
10. Prepare egg yolk batter (page 20) for colourful chiffon pops. Divide batter equally among 4 bowls and add a different gel food colouring to each bowl. Mix well.
11. Prepare meringue (page 20) for colourful chiffon pops. Divide meringue into 4 equal portions. Gently fold a portion of meringue into each egg yolk batter one-third at a time.
12. Spoon pink, yellow and blue batters into 3–4 cake pop cavities each. Bake at 160°C for 12 minutes. Leave to cool before unmoulding.
13. Pour remaining yellow batter into prepared 15-cm baking pan. Bake at 160°C for 15 minutes. Invert sheet cake onto a sheet of baking paper and let cool.
14. Peel baking paper from sheet cake and place on a cutting mat. Use a 6-cm round cutter to cut 15 circles from mint sheet cakes and 2 circles from dark chocolate sheet cake. Adhere to top of cupcakes using marshmallow cream.
15. Arrange cupcakes into the shape of a Christmas tree. Use a star cutter to cut a star from yellow sheet cake. Adhere star to apex of Christmas tree using marshmallow cream.
16. Decorate Christmas tree with colourful cake pops and adhere using marshmallow cream.
17. Use string candy to complete decorating Christmas tree.

Reduced Egg Yolk Vanilla Snowman Cake

Makes one 33-cm x 15-cm cake

Recipe on pages 116 and 117

Reduced egg yolk vanilla chiffon

Egg yolk batter

1 egg yolk

20 g castor sugar

40 g corn/vegetable oil

45 g water

1 tsp vanilla extract

60 g cake flour, sifted

White food colouring (optional)

Meringue

4 egg whites

45 g castor sugar

1/4 tsp cream of tartar

1. Preheat oven to 160°C. Prepare a 15-cm ball cake pan and a 11-cm round glass bowl.
2. Prepare egg yolk batter (page 20) and meringue (page 20) for reduced egg yolk vanilla chiffon. Gently fold meringue into egg yolk batter one-third at a time.
3. Pour batter into ball pan and glass bowl until both are about three-quarters full. Gently tap pan and bowl on counter top to release any air bubbles.
4. Bake pan at 160°C for 15 minutes, 150°C for 15 minutes, then 140°C for 5–10 minutes, or until a skewer inserted into the centre of cake comes out clean. Bake bowl at 160°C for 15 minutes, then 150°C for 15 minutes.
5. Invert pan and bowl on a wire rack to cool completely before unmoulding. (If either cake rises over the top of the mould, wait a while for it to shrink before inverting the mould.)

Vanilla chiffon

Egg yolk batter

2 egg yolks

13 g castor sugar

26 g corn/vegetable oil

27 g water

3 g vanilla extract

40 g cake flour, sifted

Orange and pink gel food colouring

1/2 tsp charcoal powder

1/2 tsp red yeast powder mixed with a pinch of baking powder, or red gel food colouring

Meringue

3 egg whites

30 g castor sugar

1/4 tsp cream of tartar

Finishing

Marshmallow cream (page 27)

6. Preheat oven to 160°C. Prepare an 11-cm round glass bowl, a silicone cake pop mould with 3-cm cavities and a paper cone placed in a small glass bowl to keep it upright. Line a 23-cm baking pan with baking paper.
7. Prepare egg yolk batter (page 20) for vanilla chiffon. Spoon 2 tsp batter into a small bowl and add a little orange gel food colouring for orange batter. Divide remaining batter into 3 equal portions (approximately 6 tsp or 2 Tbsp per portion). Add charcoal powder to one portion for black batter. Add red yeast powder mixture or a little red gel food colouring to the second portion for red batter. Add a little pink gel food colouring to the third portion for a pink batter. Mix well.
8. Prepare meringue (page 20) for vanilla chiffon. Gently fold meringue into respective egg yolk batters one-third at a time: 4 Tbsp meringue into orange batter, 12 Tbsp meringue each into black, red and pink batters.
9. Pour some red batter into prepared bowl until half full. Spoon remaining red batter into a cavity in cake pop mould. Bake bowl at 160°C for 15 minutes, then 150°C for another 15 minutes. Bake cake pop at 160°C for 12 minutes. Leave cakes on a wire rack to cool completely before unmoulding.
10. Spoon orange batter into paper cone until one-third full. Bake cone at 160°C for 15 minutes or until a skewer inserted into the centre of cake comes out clean. Leave cone to cool completely before unmoulding.
11. Pour pink and black batters side by side into prepared baking pan. Bake at 160°C for 15 minutes. Invert sheet cake onto a sheet of baking paper and let cool.
12. To assemble, apply marshmallow cream on top of ball cake and position white bowl cake over for head of snowman. Apply marshmallow cream on top of white bowl cake and place red bowl cake over for snowman's cap. Apply marshmallow cream on red cake pop and place on red bowl cake to complete cap.
13. Peel baking paper from sheet cake. Use a round cutter to cut 2 circles for eyes from black sheet cake and 2 circles for buttons from pink sheet cake. Use the round cutter to cut a mouth by making 2 cuts 1 mm apart on black sheet cake. Use a knife to cut two 2-cm thick strips from pink sheet cake for snowman's scarf. Adhere parts to snowman using marshmallow cream.
14. Trim orange cone cake to about 1 cm long for snowman's nose. Adhere to snowman using marshmallow cream.

Pineapple Tart Cake

Makes one 23-cm cake

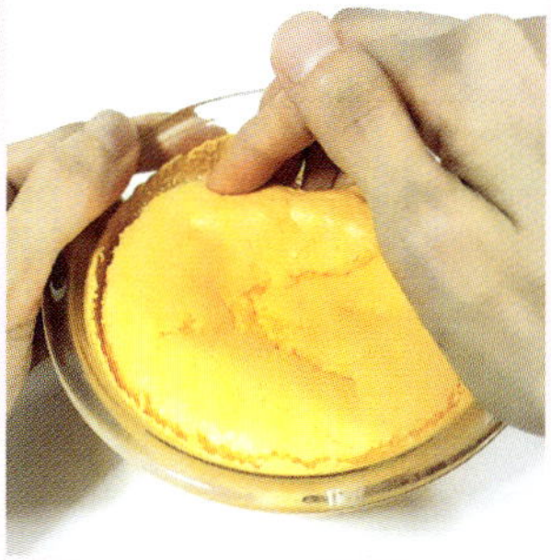

Egg yolk batter

3 egg yolks

18 g castor sugar

38 g vegetable/corn oil

48 g pineapple juice

60 g cake flour, sifted

Orange gel food colouring

Meringue

4 egg whites

45 g castor sugar

1/4 tsp cream of tartar

Finishing

Marshmallow cream (page 27)

1. Preheat oven to 160°C. Prepare a 23-cm silicone Bundt pan and an 11-cm round glass bowl. Line a 15-cm square baking pan with baking paper.
2. Prepare egg yolk batter (page 20). Spoon 10 tsp batter into another bowl. Add a little orange gel food colouring and mix well for orange batter.
3. Prepare meringue (page 20). Gently fold meringue one-third at a time into respective egg yolk batters: 20 Tbsp meringue into orange batter and remaining meringue into remaining plain batter.
4. Pour plain batter into Bundt pan until batter is about 3 cm high. Pour orange batter into bowl until bowl is three-quarters full.
5. Bake at 160°C for 15 minutes, 150°C for 10 minutes, then 140°C for 5–10 minutes, or until a skewer inserted into the centre of cakes comes out clean.
6. Pour remaining plain batter into prepared baking pan. Bake sheet cake at 160°C for 15 minutes. Invert sheet cake onto a sheet of baking paper and let cool.
7. To assemble, place orange bowl cake into depression of Bundt cake. Cut two short strips from sheet cake to complete look of pineapple tart. Adhere using marshmallow cream.

Mandarin Orange Ji Cake

Makes one 18-cm cake

Recipe on pages 122 and 123

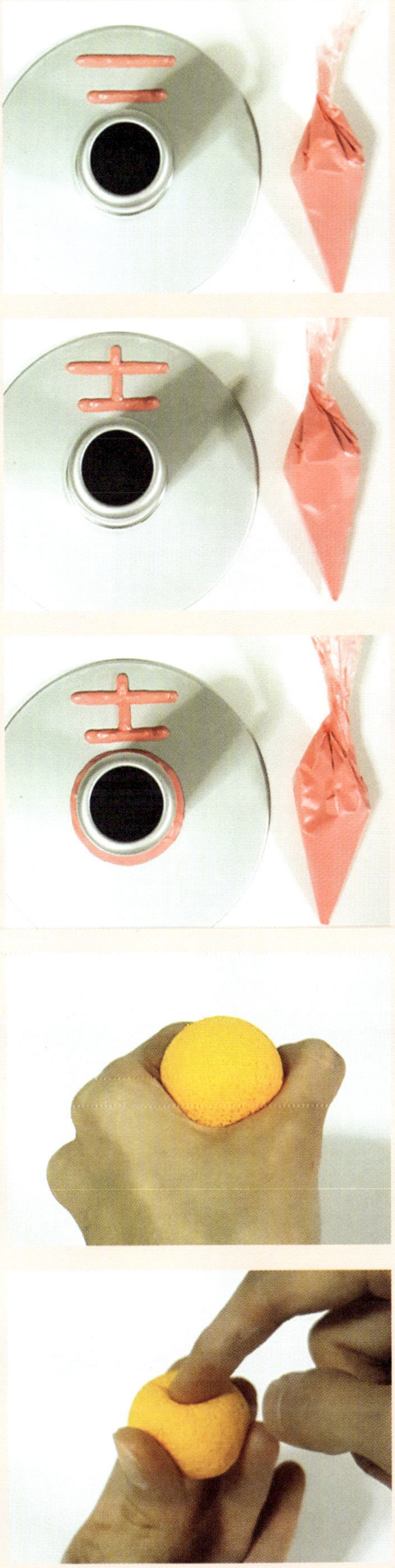

Mandarin orange chiffon

Egg yolk batter

3 egg yolks

20 g castor sugar

38 g vegetable/corn oil

47 g mandarin orange juice

Zest from 1 1/2 mandarin oranges

60 g cake flour, sifted

A few drops of orange emulco

1/4 tsp red yeast powder mixed with a pinch of baking powder, or red gel food colouring

Meringue for pattern batter

1 egg white

1/5 tsp cream of tartar

11 g castor sugar

Meringue for cake batter

4 egg whites

1/4 tsp cream of tartar

45 g castor sugar

1. Preheat oven to 160°C. Prepare an 18-cm chiffon tube pan.
2. Prepare egg yolk batter (page 20) for mandarin orange chiffon. Spoon 2 tsp batter into a small bowl for pattern batter. Add red yeast powder mixture or a little red gel food colouring for red batter. Mix well.
3. Prepare meringue (page 20) for pattern batter. Gently fold 7 Tbsp meringue into red batter one-third at a time.
4. Spoon red batter into a disposable piping bag and cut a 3-mm hole at the tip. Pipe the Chinese character 吉 on the base of the tube pan. Pipe 2 horizontal strokes, a vertical stroke across and a ring around the tube, rotating the pan as you go. (The batter needs to be 3–5 mm thick for it to adhere to the cake when unmoulded.)
5. Bake pattern at 160°C for 1.5 minutes. Set aside.
6. Prepare meringue (page 20) for cake batter. Gently fold meringue into remaining mandarin orange chiffon batter one-third at a time.
7. Pour cake batter into tube pan until batter is about 2 cm from rim of pan. Gently tap pan on counter top to release any air bubbles.
8. Bake at 160°C for 15 minutes, then 140°C for 30 minutes, or until a skewer inserted into the centre of cake comes out clean.

Kumquat chiffon

Egg yolk batter

2 egg yolks

13 g castor sugar

25 g vegetable/corn oil

30 g mandarin orange juice

Zest from 1 mandarin orange

40 g cake flour, sifted

A few drops of orange emulco

Green gel food colouring

Meringue

3 egg whites

1/4 tsp cream of tartar

30 g castor sugar

Finishing

Marshmallow cream (page 27)

9. Invert pan on a wire rack to cool completely before unmoulding.
10. Preheat oven to 160°C. Prepare a silicone cake pop mould with 3-cm cavities. Line a 20-cm square baking pan with baking paper.
11. Prepare egg yolk batter (page 20) for kumquat chiffon. Spoon 9 tsp or 3 Tbsp batter into another bowl. Add a little green gel food colouring for green batter. Mix well. Leave other portion orange.
12. Prepare meringue (page 20) for kumquat chiffon. Gently fold meringue into respective batters one-third at a time: 18 Tbsp meringue into green batter and remaining meringue for orange batter. Spoon orange batter into 10 cavities in cake pop mould. Bake at 160°C for 12 minutes. Leave to cool completely before unmoulding.
13. Pour green batter into prepared baking pan. Bake at 160°C for 15 minutes. Invert sheet cake onto a sheet of baking paper and let cool.
14. Peel baking paper from sheet cake and place on a cutting mat. Use a leaf cutter to cut 8–10 leaves from green sheet cake. Use a mini flower or star cutter to cut 10 calyxes.
15. To form a kumquat, cup base of a cake pop in one hand to shape it. Apply a dot of marshmallow cream on cake pop and add a calyx. Press it down using your finger. Stick leaves on using marshmallow cream. Repeat with remaining cake pops.
16. Place kumquat on cake in clusters and adhere using marshmallow cream.

Peanut Butter & Jam Iced Gems Chiffon Cakes

Makes three 11-cm cakes

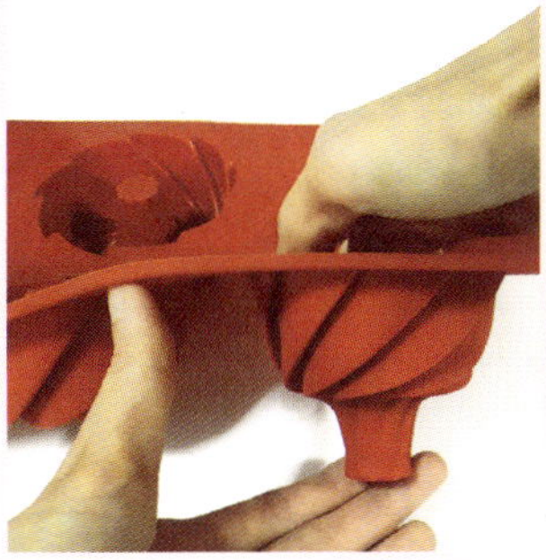

Egg yolk batter
3 egg yolks

20 g castor sugar

39 g vegetable/corn oil

42 g water

1 tsp vanilla extract

60 g cake flour, sifted

1/4 tsp baking powder

A pinch of salt

1 tsp strawberry jam + a few drops of strawberry paste

1 tsp kaya + a little green gel food colouring (optional)

1 tsp apricot jam

22 g peanut butter

1/4 tsp baking soda

Meringue
4 egg whites

1/4 tsp cream of tartar

45 g castor sugar

Finishing
Marshmallow cream (page 27)

1. Preheat oven to 160°C. Prepare a silicone Bundt mould with six 7.5-cm cavities. Push tube in each cavity down to create shape for icing. Place each cavity into a cut paper cone for support, then place mould into a baking pan for additional support. Skip this step if you have a mould in the right shape. Prepare three 11-cm round glass bowls.
2. Prepare egg yolk batter (page 20). Spoon 5 tsp batter each into 3 small bowls. Add strawberry jam and strawberry paste to one bowl. Add kaya and green gel food colouring to second bowl. Add apricot jam to third bowl. Add peanut butter and baking soda to remaining batter. Mix well.
3. Prepare meringue (page 20). Gently fold meringue into respective batters one-third at a time: 10 Tbsp meringue each into strawberry, kaya and apricot batters and remaining meringue into peanut butter batter.
4. Pour strawberry, kaya and apricot batters into separate cavities in Bundt mould until about two-thirds full. Pour peanut butter batter equally into glass bowls until bowls are two-thirds full.
5. Bake Bundt cakes at 160°C for 15 minutes, then 150°C for 10 minutes, or until a skewer inserted into the centre of cakes comes out clean. Bake bowls at 160°C for 15 minutes, then 150°C for 15 minutes, or until a skewer inserted into the centre of cakes comes out clean.
6. Leave cakes on a wire rack to cool completely before unmoulding.
7. Round up base of peanut butter chiffon by cupping base of cakes with your hands. Use a knife to make cuts around sides of cake to complete look of biscuit.
8. Pinch tips of Bundt cakes to resemble icing.
9. Apply marshmallow cream on top of each peanut butter chiffon and place strawberry, kaya and apricot Bundt cakes over.

Pumpkin Monster Cake

Makes one 15-cm cake

Recipe on pages 128 and 129

Pumpkin chiffon

Egg yolk batter

80 g pumpkin, cut into small cubes

3 egg yolks

18 g castor sugar

40 g vegetable/corn oil

11 g water/milk

60 g cake flour, sifted

A pinch of salt

Meringue

4 egg whites

$^1/_4$ tsp cream of tartar

45 g castor sugar

1. Prepare pumpkin purée. Steam pumpkin until cooked and soft. Mash pumpkin into a purée. Measure out 60 g purée for use in pumpkin chiffon.
2. Preheat oven to 160°C. Prepare a 15-cm chiffon tube pan and a silicone cake pop mould with 3-cm cavities. Line a 15-cm square baking pan with baking paper.
3. Prepare egg yolk batter (page 20) and meringue (page 20) for pumpkin chiffon. Gently fold meringue into egg yolk batter one-third at a time.
4. Pour batter into tube pan until batter is about 2 cm from rim of pan. Gently tap pan on counter top to release any air bubbles.
5. Bake at 160°C for 15 minutes, then 140°C for 20–25 minutes, or until a skewer inserted into the centre of cake comes out clean.
6. Spoon remaining batter into 3 cavities in cake pop mould and prepared baking pan. Bake cake pops at 160°C for 12 minutes and pan for 15 minutes, or until a skewer inserted into the centre of cake comes out clean.
7. Invert tube pan on a wire rack to cool completely before unmoulding. Leave cake pops to cool completely before unmoulding. Invert sheet cake onto a sheet of baking paper and let cool.

Eye cake pops and sheet cakes

Egg yolk batter

1 egg yolk

10 g castor sugar

21 g vegetable/corn oil

22 g water

3 g vanilla extract

30 g cake flour, sifted

Pink gel food colouring

1/2 tsp charcoal powder

Meringue

2 egg whites

1/8 tsp cream of tartar

23 g castor sugar

Finishing

Marshmallow cream (page 27)

8. Preheat oven to 160°C. Prepare a silicone cake pop mould with 3-cm cavities. Line a 20-cm square baking pan with baking paper.
9. Prepare egg yolk batter (page 20) for eye cake pops and sheet cakes. Spoon 3 tsp batter into a small bowl and leave plain. Spoon 3 tsp batter into another bowl and add a little pink gel food colouring for pink batter. Add charcoal powder to remaining batter for a black batter. Mix well.
10. Prepare meringue (page 20) for eye pops and sheet cakes. Gently fold meringue into respective batters one-third at a time: 6 Tbsp meringue each into plain and pink batters and remainder into black batter.
11. Spoon plain batter equally into 3 cavities in cake pop mould. Bake at 160°C for 12 minutes.
12. Pour black and pink batters side by side into prepared baking pan. Gently tap pan on counter top to release any air bubbles. Bake at 160°C for 14–15 minutes. Invert sheet cake onto a sheet of baking paper and let cool.
13. Peel baking paper from pumpkin sheet cake and place on a cutting mat. Use a medium round cutter to cut a circle to cover hole in pumpkin chiffon. Fill centre of cake marshmallows or sweets for a hidden surprise, then conceal it with the circle cut-out.
14. Place cake pops on a cutting mat. Use a circle cutter to make a similar cut on pumpkin and plain cake pops to create eyeballs. Use marshmallow cream to join larger half a pumpkin cake pop to smaller half of a plain cake pop to form eyelids and eyeballs. Insert a straw into eyeballs. Set aside.
15. Peel baking paper from black and pink sheet cake and place on a cutting mat. Use a large oval cutter to cut an oval from black sheet cake, then use another oval cutter to cut out a smile. Use a small round cutter to cut eyes from black sheet cake.
16. Use a small round cutter to cut a circle from pink sheet cake, then make a slit at one corner for the tongue.
17. Assemble parts using marshmallow cream. Insert cake pop eyeballs into top of cake.

Raspberry Jelly Surprise Flower Cake

Makes one 18-cm cake

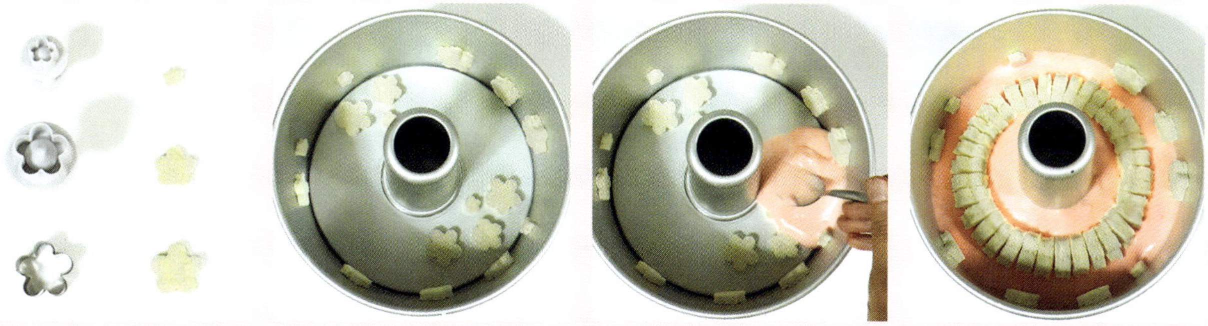

Vanilla sheet cake

Egg yolk batter

2 egg yolks
14 g castor sugar
26 g vegetable/corn oil
34 g water
40 g cake flour, sifted

Meringue

3 egg whites
1/4 tsp cream of tartar
30 g castor sugar

Jelly chiffon

Egg yolk batter

3 egg yolks
40 g vegetable/corn oil
47 g milk
65 g cake flour, sifted
26 g raspberry jelly powder
1/4 tsp baking powder

Meringue

4 egg whites
45 g castor sugar
1/4 tsp cream of tartar

1. Preheat oven to 160°C. Line a 25-cm square baking pan with baking paper.
2. Prepare egg yolk batter (page 20) and meringue (page 20) for vanilla sheet cake. Gently fold meringue into batter one-third at a time.
3. Pour batter onto prepared baking pan. Gently tap on counter top to release any air bubbles.
4. Bake sheet cake at 160°C for 15 minutes. Invert sheet cake onto a sheet of baking paper and let cool.
5. Peel baking paper from sheet cake and place on a cutting mat. Use flower cutters of various sizes to cut out a few flowers to decorate the base and sides of cake.
6. Use a 3-cm flower cutter to cut about 36 flowers to form a ring of flowers for the surprise.
7. Preheat oven to 160°C. Prepare a 15-cm chiffon tube pan.
8. Prepare egg yolk batter (page 20) and meringue (page 20) for jelly chiffon. Gently fold meringue into batter one-third at a time.
9. Arrange flowers for decoration on base and sides of tube pan, making sure that the moist, sticky side faces pan. (This is the top of the sheet cake.)
10. Spoon some jelly batter over flowers on base of pan until batter is about 2 cm thick. Arrange ring of flowers in pan, lining them up as closely as possible. Gently pour remaining batter over to cover ring of flowers as well as flowers at the side of pan.
11. Bake at 160°C for 15 minutes, then 140°C for 31 minutes, or until a skewer inserted into the centre of cake comes out clean.
12. Invert pan on wire rack to cool completely before unmoulding.
13. Slice to cake to reveal the hidden surprise!

Weights & Measures

Weight of Ingredients

1 egg (with shell) = 60 g

1 egg (without shell) = 53 g

1 egg yolk = 13 g

1 egg white = 40 g

1 tsp egg yolk batter = 5 g

1 Tbsp egg yolk batter = 15 g

2 Tbsp meringue = 5 g

1 Tbsp cake flour = 6.25 g

1 Tbsp castor sugar = 14 g

1 Tbsp cocoa powder = 7.38 g

A pinch of salt/baking powder = $^{1}/_{8}$ tsp

1 Tbsp vegetable oil = 14 g

1 Tbsp water/milk/most liquids = 15 g

Standard Conversions

Liquid and Volume Measures

3 tsp = 1 Tbsp = $^{1}/_{2}$ fl oz = 15 ml

16 Tbsp = 1 cup = 8 fl oz = 250 ml

Dry Measures

30 g = 1 oz

100 g = 3$^{1}/_{2}$ oz

280 g = 10 oz

Length

0.5 cm = $^{1}/_{4}$ inch

1 cm = $^{1}/_{2}$ inch

1.5 cm = $^{3}/_{4}$ inch

2.5 cm = 1 inch

Number of Egg Yolks Needed by Pan Size

15-cm chiffon tube pan = 2 egg yolks

18-cm chiffon tube pan = 3 egg yolks

20-cm chiffon tube pan = 4 egg yolks

23-cm chiffon tube pan = 6 egg yolks

Chiffon Tube Pan Size Conversions for Single Tone Cakes

To scale up from a 15-cm pan to an 18-cm pan, divide quantities by 2, then multiply by 3.

To scale up from an 18-cm pan to a 20-cm pan, divide quantities by 3, then multiply by 4.

To scale up from an 18-cm pan to a 23-cm pan, divide quantities by 3, then multiply by 6.

Oven Temperature Conversions

130°C = 265°F

140°C = 285°F

150°C = 300°F

160°C = 325°F

Abbreviations Used

tsp	teaspoon
Tbsp	tablespoon
g	gram
kg	kilogram
ml	milliliter